25 Bicycle Tours in New Jersey

Over 900 Miles of Scenic Pleasures and Historic Treasures

by Arline Zatz and Joel Zatz

Backcountry Publications
Woodstock, Vermont

To our parents, who set us in motion

An invitation to the reader
Although it is unlikely that the roads you cycle on these tours will change much with time, some road signs, landmarks, and other items may. If you find that changes have occurred on these routes, please let us know so we may correct them in future editions. The author and publisher also welcome other comments and suggestions. Address all correspondence:

Editor, *Bicycle Tours*
Backcountry Publications
P.O. Box 175
Woodstock, Vermont 05091

Library of Congress Cataloging-in-Publication Data
Zatz, Arline, 1937-
    25 bicycle tours in New Jersey   :   over 900 miles of scenic
pleasures and historic treasures   /   by Arline Zatz and Joel Zatz.
        p.   cm.
    Includes index.
    ISBN 0-942440-42-0 (pbk.)
    1. Bicycle touring—New Jersey—Guide-books. 2. New Jersey—Description and travel—1981- —Guide-books. I. Zatz, Joel L.,
1935-   . II. Title. III. Title: Twenty-five bicycle tours in New
Jersey.
GV1045.5.N5Z37 1988   87-34922
917.49'0443—dc 19   CIP

© 1988 by Arline and Joel Zatz
First edition: fourth printing, 1991, updated.
All rights reserved
Published by Backcountry Publications
A division of The Countryman Press, Inc.
Woodstock, VT 05091
Printed in the United States of America

Text and cover design by Richard Widhu
Maps by Richard Widhu, © 1988 Backcountry Publications
Photographs by the authors
Cover photograph taken at Wheaton Village by Arline Zatz

Acknowledgments

We wish to express our sincere appreciation to our son, David, for reading our manuscript and offering his frank appraisal and helpful suggestions.

We are grateful to Sarah Spiers for carefully editing our words and checking our routes; to our publisher, Christopher Lloyd, for his advice, flexibility, and optimism; to Marcia and Seymour Greenwald for accompanying us on some of the tours; and to Laura and Marvin Mausner for sharing their favorite bike route with us.

We also thank William Feldman, the New Jersey Department of Transportation Bicycle Advocate; Don and Violet Curley; the Hunterdon County Park System; the Cape May Planning Board; the Ocean County Parks Department; and the Bergen County Office of Historic and Cultural Affairs.

Arline extends a special heartfelt note of thanks to Felicia Oliver-Smith for her encouragement and support.

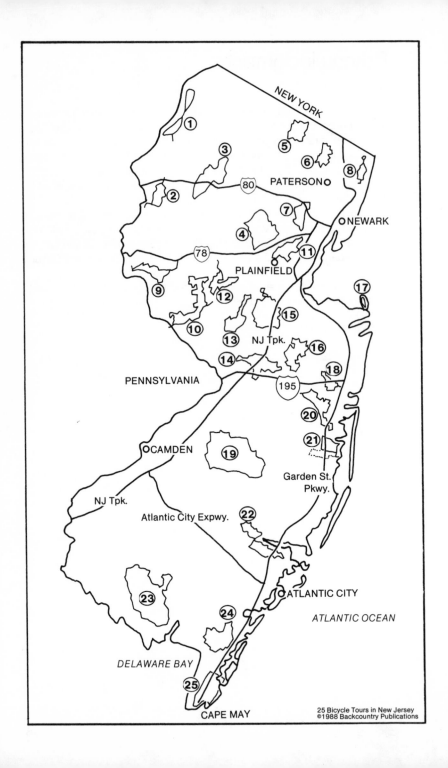

NEW YORK

① ③ ⑤

⑥ ⑧

80 PATERSON○

② ⑦

○NEWARK

④ 78 ⑪

PLAINFIELD ⑰

⑨ ⑫ ⑮

⑩ ⑬ NJ Tpk. ⑯

⑭ ⑱

PENNSYLVANIA 195

⑳

㉑

○CAMDEN ⑲ Garden St.
Pkwy.

NJ Tpk.

Atlantic City Expwy. ㉒

㉓ ○ATLANTIC CITY

㉔ ATLANTIC OCEAN

DELAWARE BAY

㉕

CAPE MAY

25 Bicycle Tours in New Jersey
©1988 Backcountry Publications

Contents

Introduction

With an estimated three million cyclists in New Jersey, it's easy to understand why bicycling is the state's most popular form of outdoor recreation. Not only does bicycling reduce stress by refreshing the mind, but it improves the cardiovascular system, tones the muscles, builds strength and endurance, and is simply fun.

The 25 tours we've laid out cover over 900 miles and explore many of the treasures and delights in the state. No matter which tour you choose, you'll discover New Jersey's great diversity. You can view the state's largest lake in the hilly, northern Skylands section, but if you want leisurely pedaling and a perfect example of why New Jersey is known as the "Garden State," try a tour through the southern flatlands. The routes traverse lush forests, miles of white sandy beaches, lovely neighborhoods, and natural areas and lead you to historic sites, museums, and wildlife refuges. You can rest or fish in the same babbling brooks and flowing rivers the Lenni-Lenape Indians used, and you will sometimes find yourself pedaling on the same roads General George Washington and his troops travelled upon.

To make it easier to choose a tour, the book is divided geographically into three sections—north, central, and south. Trip highlights and information on the county, starting point, terrain, traffic conditions, and distance are listed at the beginning of each tour. You can see at a glance how difficult the trip is and what you're going to encounter along the way. While two of these tours are overnighters, all are circular and each can be shortened or completed in sections.

WHO THESE TOURS ARE FOR

Whether you ride at a snail's pace or are as fast as a jaguar, whether you're a beginner or experienced cyclist, you'll find tours to match your abilities and interests. In choosing a tour, check the terrain rating and mileage from start to finish. If you're out of shape, begin with short, level trips (or parts of longer trips) until you feel comfortable enough to try more difficult ones. By bicycling a couple of times a week, you'll find your ability to venture on slightly hilly terrain has greatly improved.

THE TOUR

Read each tour carefully a few days before starting out so you can plan how long to allow for lingering at museums, historic sites, swimming and fishing areas, etc., and what to bring along.

Each tour has turn-by-turn instructions, running mileage, and a map showing points of interest. Local attractions, rest rooms, food stops, and nearby bicycle repair shops are noted in the text. All attractions are fully described so you can prepare your schedule before you start out. Business hours are given, but since they may change, it's a good idea to call in advance.

Detailed street maps of each county are available free or at a nominal charge from the respective county offices. Write to the New Jersey Department of Transportation, Pedestrian/Bicycle Unit, 1035 Parkway Avenue, Trenton, N.J. 08625, for a listing.

IT'S THE LAW

While bicyclists aren't bogged down by many rules, New Jersey does require that you follow the same rules of the road as car drivers do. In addition to giving hand signals, obeying stop signs, traffic lights, and other warnings, the law states that:

• Cyclists remain on the right side of the road except when making a left turn from a left-turn lane, when avoiding drains or other hazardous conditions, or passing a slower moving vehicle.
• A red rear reflector and front and rear lights must be used after sunset.
• A bell or horn which can be heard for at least 100 feet must be attached to the bicycle. Sirens or whistles, however, are illegal.

Bicycles are not allowed on the Garden State Parkway, New Jersey Turnpike, or the Atlantic City Expressway. While interstates in New Jersey are closed to bicyclists, most sections may be used by writing for a special permit issued by the New Jersey Department of Transportation (NJDOT), c/o William Feldman, Pedestrian/Bicyle Advocate, New Jersey Department of Transportation, 1035 Parkway Avenue, Trenton, N.J. 08625. However, none of our routes take you on the major highways.

SAFETY TIPS

According to a recent study of bicycle-related injuries by Seth Ruderman, M.D., of the West Jersey Health System, "Intelligent bicycling is the key to accident prevention. Proper maintenance, protective headgear, and alertness while riding would prevent many common injuries."

Always wear a helmet when you ride. You have only one head and this is its only protection. Make yourself visible by wearing bright or light-colored clothing or a simple safety vest. Always ride single file, keeping at least three bicycle lengths between you and the cyclist in front. Attach a mirror to your helmet, eyeglasses, or handlebars to avoid having to turn your head to look behind. Use a clip or rubberband to keep your pants from becoming tangled

in the chain. Use sunglasses or goggles to keep insects from flying into your eyes. Carry your bicycle across railroad tracks or cross at right angles. Test your brakes before a downhill descent. If a dog should chase you, get off your bicycle and use it as a shield. Some cyclists have had success by throwing a cookie off into the distance to distract the dog long enough to make a getaway.

BEFORE EACH TRIP

- Inspect and tighten nuts and bolts.
- Check the tire pressure.
- Adjust the brakes and check the derailleur adjustment.

WHAT TO TAKE

- Tool kit, spare tube and patch kit, tire irons, gauge, and tire pump.
- Lock and chain. Master Lock makes sturdy locks and cables; if weight and price aren't factors, the chainless Kryptonite or Citadel are good bets.
- Filled water bottle.
- Cycling gloves to absorb road shock and protect your hands in case of a fall.
- Snacks and/or lunch.
- Suntan lotion.
- Insect repellent.
- Bandana.
- Tissues.
- First-aid kit.
- Bathing suit and towel if swimming is planned.
- Money.
- Knife.
- Panniers to hold extra clothing.
- Camera and film.
- Bird and tree identification books.
- Don't forget your copy of this book.

EMERGENCY REPAIRS

Checking your bicycle before the tour is the best way to avoid a breakdown. Be familiar with the most common repairs in advance, in case the bicycle breaks down on the road. Buy a repair manual and practice repairing a flat tire or thrown chain at home. Keep a manual in your pannier should you have to make an unexpected repair. (Suggested manuals are listed in the appendix.)

NEW JERSEY TIDBITS

Length: 166 miles from High Point to Cape May
Width: 32 miles at its narrowest point
State motto: Liberty and Prosperity
State flower: Purple violet
State bird: Eastern goldfinch
State animal: The horse
State insect: Honeybee
State tree: Red oak
State nickname: Garden State

Northern New Jersey

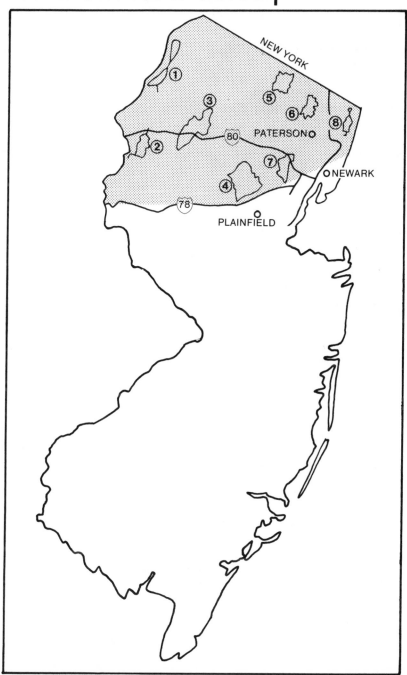

1

Old Mine Road

Location: Sussex and Warren counties
Starting point: Millbrook Village
Terrain: Hilly with some steep climbs
Traffic: Very light
Round-trip distance pedaled: 37.0 miles
Highlights: Historic Millbrook Village, scenic Delaware Water Gap region, pedaling on the first road in the nation.

Lenape Indians discovered the beautiful Delaware River Valley region thousands of years ago and made it their home. Europeans, equally impressed, followed. By the late nineteenth century, the area became a very popular place to spend a vacation.

Hikers, hunters, bird-watchers, fishermen, canoeists, and bicyclists still flock to 70,000 acres along both the Pennsylvania and New Jersey sides of the Delaware River, now known as the Delaware Water Gap National Recreation Area. The gap, a distinct notch more than a mile wide, was formed by underground pressure folding the earth's crust and the action of the Delaware River cutting through the Kittatinny Ridge. Exposed rock layers and the folding of the rocks are easily seen in many places.

The route leads through part of the gap and several quiet settlements. Except on summer weekends, traffic is light enough to enjoy the breathtaking natural beauty of the area in solitude. It's well worth the price of some strenuous pedaling in hilly terrain.

Come well supplied with food, drink, and repair tools, since stores are few and far between. It's a good idea to pick up a park map at the Delaware Water Gap National Recreation Area Visitor Center, located on Interstate 80, because many roads are unmarked or poorly marked, and town names sometimes vary from one map to another.

Park at Millbrook Village, north of the Visitor Center, and limber up by strolling through this restored crossroads hamlet. Here, National Park Service employees wear period dress and demonstrate hand crafts such as spinning, weaving, and blacksmithing, re-creating a lifestyle which was common in the Delaware River Valley only a generation ago.

The village came to life in 1832 after Abraham Garris built a dam diverting water from a brook to power the wheel of his gristmill. It didn't take long for others to realize they, too, could make a living near the mill to provide necessary services to the surrounding agricultural community. The village gristmill allowed valley farmers to grind their grain into flour without having to journey over the mountains. Millbrook flourished until 1885 when a railroad line built along the opposite side of the Kittatinny Ridge made it obsolete.

After exploring, bring your bike to the road junction at the village entrance and reset the odometer.

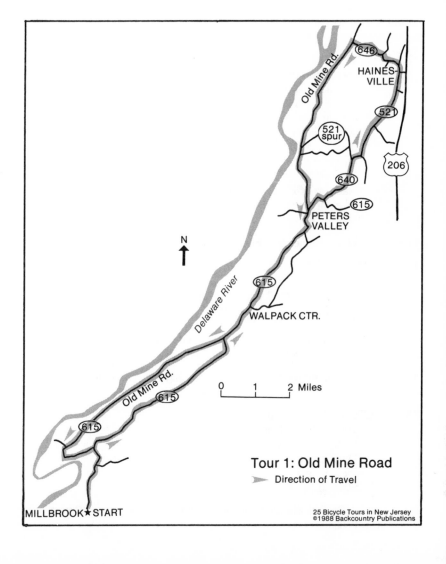

Tour 1: Old Mine Road

Direction of Travel

25 Bicycle Tours in New Jersey
©1988 Backcountry Publications

0.0   Head north on (unmarked) River Road toward the town of Walpack. (Some county maps label this Old Mine Road.)

Ĥ This narrow road climbs steeply uphill before descending sharply. Use caution.

2.1   RIGHT on Route 615, immediately after crossing a one-lane bridge.

You follow a stream for about a mile before encountering a steep section with several choppy up-and-down stretches. Trees stand out like colored lollipops during the fall, affording shade on hot days. As the countryside slopes away, you can catch glimpses of adjoining hills and valleys, continuing on through lush, green, forested areas before reaching the Old Mine Road.

7.4   RIGHT at the "T," following the main road.

There are opportunities to purchase food and drink at a store in the Walpack Valley Campground on the right just after making the turn and at the Walpack Inn on the right about half a mile down the road. After the inn there is a rangers' station on the other side of the road. As you proceed, look out to the right for a beautiful view, especially during the fall. At 11.1 miles, follow the main road to the left as an unmarked road merges from the right.

Peters Valley Craft Village, at the next road junction, is an excellent place to stop, stretch, and examine the fine crafts produced by resident artists working on their specialty. (There is no admission charge; hours are until 5 p.m. daily.)

11.9   RIGHT on Route 615, following sign for Route 206.

12.5   LEFT on Route 640 at sign for Dingman's Ferry.

There are few houses along this wooded area. Just before the next turn, you arrive at a store in the village of Layton.

13.8   RIGHT on Route 521 spur.

14.1   LEFT on Route 521 North, toward Hainesville.

The road starts uphill, then flattens out.

17.2   LEFT on unmarked Route 646 at the sign for Old Mine Road.

You pass several farms before beginning a steep downhill section.

18.8   LEFT on Old Mine Road at the "T."

The Old Mine Road, built in the mid-seventeenth century, was the first road in the United States. Covering 140 miles, it was built by the Dutch to transport ore from the Pahaquarry copper mine to Esopus (now Kingston) on the Hudson River. From here it was shipped to Holland for smelting.

22.1   STRAIGHT at the junction with Route 521 spur, toward Peters Valley Craft Village.

For about a mile this scenic road climbs steeply, but there's relief in the downhill portion which takes you back to the road junction in Peters Valley.

23.8 STRAIGHT on Route 615 toward Walpack.

28.4 STRAIGHT ahead just past the Walpack Valley Campground onto Old Mine Road.
A marker at 33.7 miles commemorates the building of the Old Mine Road.

34.9 RIGHT across the one-lane bridge.
Continue uphill for about 0.6 mile.

37.0 ARRIVE at the entrance to Millbrook Village.

Bicycle shops:
None on this route.

Journey back in time at Millbrook Village, a restored crossroads hamlet on the Old Mine Road where employees don period dress and demonstrate crafts.

2

A Bit of Hope

Location: Warren County
Starting point: Route 521, just north of Interstate 80
Terrain: Hilly
Traffic: Light to moderate
Round-trip distance pedaled: 25.7 miles
Highlights: Exquisite country scenery, historic Hope Village, fishing.

This excursion through rural Warren County will take you through farming country and quiet towns along roads that wind, climb, and, inevitably, descend. In some places you'll get an inkling of what America's most populous state must have been like 50 years ago.

Begin at the parking area just north of the Interstate 80 Hope exit, which takes you onto Route 521. Make the first left turn from Route 521 north past the interchange (opposite a motorcycle dealer). If you've passed the police barracks, you've gone too far. Reset your odometer at the parking lot exit adjoining the highway.

0.0   RIGHT on Route 521 (heading south).
Hope, the first village on the route, is worth slowing down for. The Moravians, a German Protestant sect who came here from Pennsylvania in 1769, built their houses to last. Many of their attractive stone houses still stand, including the Gemeinhaus (community house), the Single Sisters Choir, previously a residence for single women, and the four-and-a-half-story stone mill that had been used for grinding grist.

1.3   RIGHT at the blinker light on Route 609.
If St. Luke's Episcopal Church is open, stop in for a look at the organ that Queen Anne donated in 1839.

4.6   LEFT on Honey Run Road.
This road is narrow, wiggly, somewhat bumpy, and nearly void of traffic.

5.5   RIGHT on Osmun Road (unmarked).
Bear right at the fork and be prepared for some hard work; the road goes steeply uphill for about 1.2 miles.

6.9   LEFT at the "T" on (unmarked) Baylor Road.
Practically free of traffic, Baylor Road climbs steeply at first; soon after

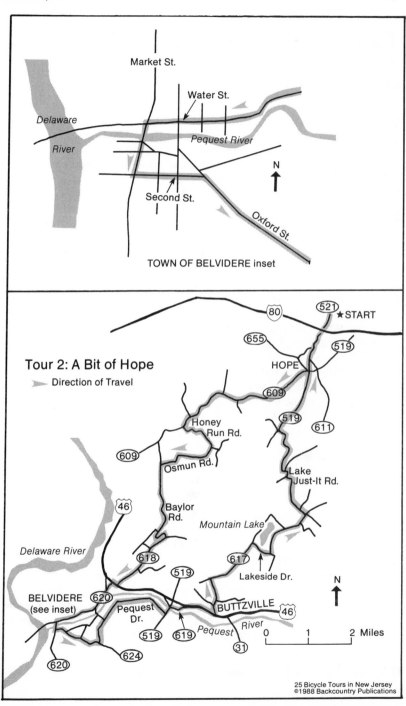

TOWN OF BELVIDERE inset

Tour 2: A Bit of Hope

Direction of Travel

25 Bicycle Tours in New Jersey
©1988 Backcountry Publications

a beautiful valley vista about a mile ahead, you'll be rewarded by a downhill section. Use caution as you come to a sharp S-curve at the foot of the hill.

8.8 **RIGHT at the "T" on Route 618 toward Belvidere.**
Cows graze lazily right next to this narrow road.

10.3 **RIGHT on Route 46, then take the first LEFT on Route 620 toward Belvidere.**
Use extreme caution entering and crossing Route 46; this is a busy artery with fast-moving traffic. After about a mile, Route 620 undergoes a name change to Water Street as it takes you into Belvidere, the county seat, established in 1825.

12.1 **LEFT on Market Street.**

12.3 **LEFT on Second Street.**
In about 0.1 mile you'll come to the town square. An attractive park is on the right and an impressive county court house is on the left. You may wish to stop for refreshments before exploring the area on foot or by bicycle. Three attractive churches, some municipal buildings, and several interesting, older homes face the park. The Robeson Mansion, standing at Second and Mansfield Streets, dominates the square. Built in the Federal style in 1834 by John Paterson Bryan Maxwell, it once hosted presidents, cabinet members, and important families in Warren County's history. Today it houses the Warren County Guidance Center. For ice cream and a rest room, try the ice-cream shop on Front Street, which runs parallel to Second Street and is 0.1 mile to the north. When you're ready, continue east on Second Street.

12.6 **RIGHT at the "T" on Oxford Street.**

13.5 **LEFT on Pequest Drive.**
This narrow, uphill stretch travels through farm country.

15.8 **LEFT at the "T" on Route 519 and cross the bridge.**

15.9 **RIGHT after the bridge on Titman Road.**

16.4 **RIGHT (east) on Route 46.**
Use extreme caution on this busy highway. The sparkling, fast flowing Pequest River, well stocked with trout, is on your right. After about 0.3 mile, you'll come to Hot Dog Johnny's, an institution for ice cream, birch beer, buttermilk, french fries, and, of course, hot dogs. Enjoy the view of the river as you relax with your snack. Rest rooms and water are available. Then, continue east on Route 46.

17.0 **LEFT on Route 617 in the town of Butzville.**

You'll feel like you're on a roller coaster on this stretch as you pass horse rental farms about 1.6 miles up the road.

19.1   RIGHT at the sign for Mountain Lake on Lakeside Drive.

You'll find rest rooms and food as you circle this small lake surrounded by houses. Continue straight ahead as a road from the west side of the lake joins in on the left.

20.8   LEFT on Lake Just-It Road.

This is a winding, narrow, hilly paved road with loose gravel on the side. The many trees and shrubs on both sides of the road provide excellent shade on a hot summer's day.

22.9   RIGHT (north) on Route 519.

24.4   STRAIGHT ahead at the flashing light on Route 521.

Arrive at the parking lot entrance on the left at 25.7 miles.

Bicycle shops:

Wheelmasters' Bicycle Shop, 12 Hardwick Street, Belvidere, (908) 475-5658.

The impressive Warren County Court House stands at the town square.

3

Allamuchy

Location: Sussex, Warren, and Morris counties
Starting point: A & P, Andover
Terrain: Hilly with some steep ascents
Traffic: Moderate
Round-trip distance pedaled: 44.2 miles
Highlights: Swimming, fishing, historic Waterloo Village, Morris Canal lock, scenic river, lakes and ponds.

Toss a bathing suit and towel in your saddlebag. This trip meanders through the hills of the Allamuchy region and visits several lakes where there are numerous opportunities for swimming and fishing, as well as many places to relax where the water sounds like music as it tumbles over rocks.

A highlight of the trip is Waterloo Village. Steeped in history, Waterloo was a favorite camping spot of the Lenni-Lenape Indians. In the 1830s, settlers enjoyed prosperity here after the Morris Canal was completed. An engineering miracle, the canal carried Pennsylvania anthracite to Andover Furnace and Andover Forge, the original name of the village. Now an historic site, it has been restored to the way it looked during the early nineteenth century.

Try for an early start and avoid summer weekends when traffic is heavy with people who flock from surrounding towns to the best swimming holes.

Start at the parking lot of the A & P on Route 517 in the Borough of Andover.

0.0   LEFT (north) on Route 517.

0.1   STRAIGHT on Route 613.

0.5   RIGHT on Roseville Road.
During the early morning hours a thick canopy of overhead leaves will shade you as you pedal along this hilly, traffic-free, narrow road. Cross over the one-lane bridge at 1.5 miles, bearing left at 2.3 miles. Wolf Lake is on the right; just after the railroad overpass, Roseville Pond appears on the left. Water lillies dot the surface of the lake while daylillies and daisies grow along its bank.

3.1   LEFT on Amity Road.
Another small pond is on the left at 4.4 miles before a steep 0.3-mile climb.

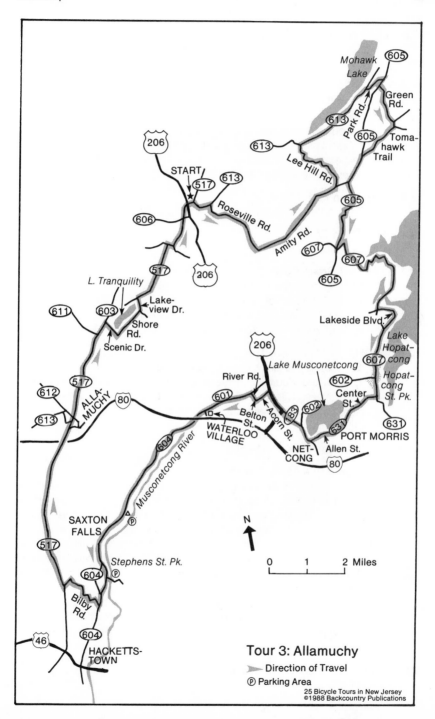

Tour 3: Allamuchy

⬤ Direction of Travel

Ⓟ Parking Area

25 Bicycle Tours in New Jersey
©1988 Backcountry Publications

5.0   LEFT on Lee Hill Road.

The road goes steeply uphill and keeps climbing for about half a mile through a newly developed housing area. You'll soon encounter a few sharp downhill curves, then a small pond on the left.

6.6   RIGHT at the "T" on Route 613, East Shore Drive.

East Shore Drive follows along the shore of Mohawk Lake, which is surrounded by a well-to-do community. Unfortunately, the appealing beach is private; for the time being, you'll have to be content watching sailboats from the road. As you cycle you may feel like you are on a roller coaster. The view along this stretch is very pleasant.

8.8   RIGHT on Park Road.

Take a deep breath; this section goes uphill all the way.

9.4   RIGHT on Route 605.

Continue uphill.

9.5   LEFT on Green Road.

Starting out uphill, this curving, extremely narrow road levels out in about 0.3 mile. Fortunately it's free of traffic and, during spring and summer months, you'll have lots of opportunities to examine a multitude of wildflowers growing along the side of the road.

10.6   RIGHT on Tomahawk Trail.

Wooded areas are slowly disappearing here as large houses are constructed. You may wish to stop at Tomahawk Lake Water Park at 11.3 miles, billed as "New Jersey's Longest Waterslide." (Open summer months; there is an admission charge. Rates are lower after 3:30 p.m.)

11.8   LEFT at the "T" on Route 605.

14.3   LEFT on Route 607 at the stop sign.

This is a sharp left turn with a steep climb for about 0.6 mile. Bear Pond is on the left at 15.1 miles. The road is quite narrow with a narrow shoulder, but there is little traffic except on summer weekends. You'll be riding along Lake Hopatcong's shoreline for awhile.

Lake Hopatcong, New Jersey's largest lake with 45 miles of shoreline, offers a large picnic area and a fine beach. All types of boats can be seen on the lake. During winter months this is an exciting place to watch ice-boat races and ice fishing. There are many opportunities to purchase food and/or drinks as you go through the town.

After passing the bridge over one arm of the lake and the marina, follow Route 607 as it turns left on Hopatchung Road (18.5 miles), then right on Lakeside Boulevard (18.7 miles).

20.0   LEFT at the entrance to Hopatcong State Park.

This is a great place to swim, rest, have lunch or a snack, or use the rest room facilities. When finished, return to the road and pick up the mileage.

20.0   LEFT on Route 607.
Use caution; traffic abounds on this four-lane, shoulderless road.

20.3   RIGHT at the sign for Port Morris.
This road, which becomes Center Street and then Allen Street, goes into Netcong. Lake Musconetcong, great for trout fishing, is visible at 21.7 miles.

22.6   RIGHT at the "T" on Route 183 (toward Newton).
Here you'll have a splendid view of the length of Lake Musconetcong. Food can be purchased at 23.1 miles just before Route 183 merges into Route 206.

24.2   LEFT on Acorn Street.
Use caution crossing Route 206. After 0.1 mile, jog to the left, then right, staying on Acorn Street.

24.7   RIGHT on Belton Street, then RIGHT on River Road.

25.0   LEFT at the "T" on Route 604, Waterloo Road.
You'll enter Allamuchy Mountain State Park at 25.2 miles. Riding in the woods along this smooth, lightly travelled road is very pleasant.

26.6   LEFT at the entrance to Waterloo Village.
Time seems to stand still at Waterloo Village. Here in this tiny hamlet situated along the Musconetcong River in a valley between the Alla-muchy and Schooley mountain ranges, you'll be transported back in time and will catch a glimpse of what the village looked like when English settlers came in the early 1700s.

The village, a living museum designed to preserve the artifacts of our Colonial roots, features working craftspersons and costumed guides. The 23 buildings filled with period furniture, objects of art, and antiques, as well as the aroma of freshly ground corn from the gristmill, will add to the sensation of being in another era. Before leaving, walk down the tree-lined path of the Morris Canal to see how the water-powered gristmill and sawmill operated. You can also pick up a free schedule of upcoming concerts held during summer months. (The village is open Tuesday to Sunday from 10 a.m. to 6 p.m., April 16 through September 30, and from 10 a.m. to 5 p.m., October 1 through December 30. There is an admission fee.)

26.6   LEFT on Route 604, Waterloo Road.
The woods and fields provide a visual treat.

29.6   LEFT into the Saxton Falls parking area (at the Morris Canal sign).

Part of Allamuchy Mountain State Park, this is the site of one of the locks of the Morris Canal which linked Phillipsburg, Pennsylvania, with Jersey City, New Jersey. Opened in 1832, the Morris Canal was the chief means of transporting anthracite coal and iron across the state. During 1866, its most prosperous year in operation, the canal carried almost 900,000 tons of freight. Dug entirely by pick and shovel, it was the first American canal built to climb hills. By way of an ingenious series of 23 inclined planes and 34 locks, 70-ton barges were set onto giant cradles and then hauled up rail tracks by chains to water levels reaching as high as 100 feet. It took five days to tow boats the canal's entire length of some 106 miles. The once highly successful canal was abandoned a century later when railroads proved a faster and less costly way to transport coal.

From this location you'll see the dam and one of the lock structures. Fly fishermen enjoy this spot, too.

31.2   LEFT at the entrance to Stephens State Park.

A short road leads to the park office. Stephens State Park is part of Allamuchy Mountain State Park and is a super place to relax, listen to bird calls, picnic at the edge of the Musconetcong River, take a short walk, fill up your canteen, or use the rest room facilities.

Lake Hopatcong, the state's largest lake, is a great place to watch ice fishing during winter months.

Limestone was extensively mined here during the latter part of the nineteenth century, and next to the office stands a kiln used to produce lime during that period. (Open daily; there is no admission charge.)

31.6 **TURN BACK onto the park entrance road.**
Follow the one-way signs. The exit road goes along the river.

32.0 **LEFT on Route 604.**

32.9 **RIGHT on Bilby Road.**
Climbing uphill through a wooded area, you'll encounter new housing developments.

33.8 **RIGHT (north) on Route 517.**
Route 517 narrows to a single lane with a shoulder. (You may wish to come back another time to explore nearby attractions; the Pequest Hatchery, Deer Lake, Wild West City.) Panther Valley's shops are on the left at about 35.7 miles, and Allamuchy Lake is on the right at about 36.5 miles. Be very careful at the intersection of Interstate 80 at about 36.9 miles; there's usually heavy traffic here. A hilly area lies ahead.

39.8 **RIGHT on Scenic Drive.**
The one-lane bridge at 40.1 miles offers a nice view of Lake Tranquility.

40.2 **LEFT on Shore Road.**
The lake is on the left.

41.0 **LEFT at the "T" on Lakeview Drive.**
This is the eastern end of Lake Tranquility.

41.2 **RIGHT on Route 517.**
Pastoral scenes are a welcome sight, followed at 32.1 miles by the last view of water on the trip—tiny Buckmire Pond. Follow Route 517 as it turns right on Whitehall Road; then go left on Decker Pond Road. Good Shepherd Catholic Church on the right has an unusual design and an impressive bell tower. Routes 517 and 206 join in Andover; stay on Route 517 as they separate.
You'll arrive at the starting point at 44.2 miles.

Bicycle shops:
Cycle Center of Andover, Route 206, Andover, (201) 786-6350.
Alpine Ski and Bike, 207 Mountain Avenue, Hackettstown, (908) 852-4422.
Lakeside Cyclery, Lakeside Boulevard, Landing, (201) 398-7836.
Route 15 Bicycle Outlet, Route 15, Lake Hopatcong, (201) 663-1935.
Bike Stop, 9 Main Street, Sparta, (201) 729-7775.

4

Jockey Hollow and Loantaka

Location: Morris County
Starting point: Jockey Hollow
Terrain: Hilly
Traffic: Light
Round-trip distance pedaled: 25.7 miles
Highlights: Jockey Hollow, Loantaka Brook County Park, Great Swamp, nature center, bird-watching.

George Washington slept in dozens of places, but his troops were probably most uncomfortable during his stay in Morristown in the bitter winter of 1779-80. Washington brought his starving, freezing, and nearly naked troops to nearby Jockey Hollow to rest because the Watchung Mountains east of town provided cover from the British army in New York City, 30 miles away, and local ironworks provided him with necessary equipment. Over the long harsh winter, his men had time to rest and reassemble; by the time spring came, the Continental Army was greatly reinforced. During this trip, you'll learn how the army survived, held together by Washington's leadership and ability. After looking at the crude huts soldiers occupied and learning how they suffered, you'll be glad to be back in the twentieth century.

After touring Morristown National Historical Park, the trip leads through tranquil Loantaka (pronounced Low on' aka) Brook County Park and then through a portion of Great Swamp National Wildlife Refuge.

The Great Swamp was bought by the English in 1708 from the Delaware Indians for a barrel of rum, 15 kettles, 4 pistols, and various other goods. Used for farming until the land was no longer productive, the swamp received national attention in 1959 when a jetport was proposed. Outraged citizens raised a million dollars to buy the land, which they later turned over to the Department of the Interior, and in 1968 Congress designated it part of the National Wilderness Preservation System. It is now a haven for hikers and bird-watchers as well as a variety of wildlife.

Park your car at the Visitor Center in the Jockey Hollow section of Morristown National Historical Park. Before starting on your trip, stop in at the Visitor Center, ask for a brochure, and spend a few minutes browsing through the displays. When finished, get your bike and set the odometer to zero at the "tour road" sign at the perimeter of the parking lot.

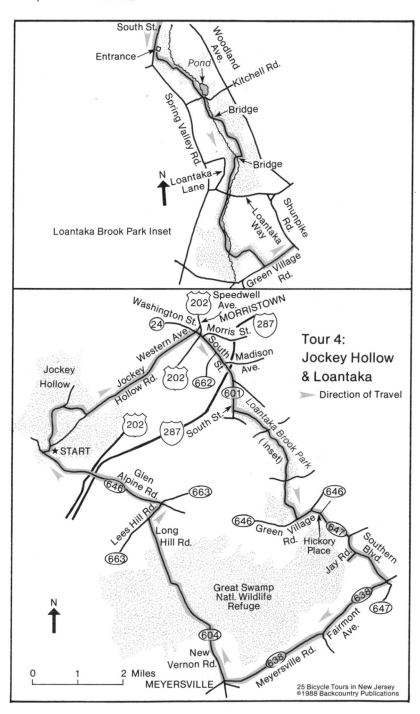

Loantaka Brook Park Inset

South St.

Woodland Ave.

Entrance

Pond

Kitchell Rd.

Bridge

Spring Valley Rd.

Bridge

N

Loantaka Lane

Shunpike Rd.

Loantaka Way

Green Village Rd.

Washington St.

202 Speedwell Ave.

MORRISTOWN

24

Morris St.

287

Western Ave.

South St.

Madison Ave.

Tour 4:
Jockey Hollow
& Loantaka

Jockey Hollow

Jockey Hollow Rd.

202

662

601

Direction of Travel

Loantaka Brook Park

202

287 South St.

(inset)

★ START

Glen Alpine Rd.

646

663

646

Lees Hill Rd.

Long Hill Rd.

646 Green Village Rd.

Hickory Place

647

Southern Blvd

663

Jay Rd.

638

647

N

Great Swamp Natl. Wildlife Refuge

Fairmont Ave.

604

New Vernon Rd.

638 Meyersville Rd.

0   1   2 Miles

MEYERSVILLE

25 Bicycle Tours in New Jersey
©1988 Backcountry Publications

0.0 STRAIGHT ahead on the tour road.

This narrow, winding road is level at first, climbing at 0.2 mile for another 0.2 mile as it passes through a forested area. Lock your bicycle at the 1.0 mile-junction, and walk up to the top of the hill to see reproductions of the crude huts used by troops of the Pennsylvania line.

The scene was bleak, with little to show that these 2000 men were the backbone of Washington's army. Many had marched in the 1775 invasion of Canada, fought the 1777 British crossing of Brandywine Creek, and advanced into enemy fire at Germantown.

1.0 RIGHT on the tour road.

This fairly smooth road with some hills follows through a wooded area before an exhibit at 1.4 miles on the left side of the road. Stop a while to read details about the life soldiers led. Military life centered around this Grand Parade area, and it was here that officers inspected troops daily. Military ceremony was as important then as it is today, and on these grounds, guards were assigned, orders issued, and punishment announced.

1.6 LEFT on Jockey Hollow Road at the sign for Morristown.

A rest room is immediately to the right of the turn. The road name eventually changes to Western Avenue. This section has some steep uphill climbs; the road is narrow, with no shoulder and many ruts. After entering Morristown and climbing a steep half mile, you'll see a sign for Fort Nonsense at 4.5 miles. It's said that Washington had his men dig trenches and raise embankments here to give them something to do, thus its name. Although nothing remains of the fort, now commemorated by a large stone tablet, the site offers an engaging vista of the surrounding town if you have energy for the extremely steep climb.

4.6 RIGHT on Washington Street.

You'll pass stores and restaurants before coming to the town square. There is heavy traffic here. Impressive St. Peter's Episcopal Church is on the right at 5.0 miles. Continue straight ahead; the street name changes to South Street. Watch for Seaton Hackney Farm Park (open daily for riding; a fee is charged) on the left. You turn just after the Farm Park.

6.6 LEFT at entrance to Loantaka Brook County Park, then an immediate RIGHT onto the bicycle path.

A nicely paved path, shared by bikers, hikers, and joggers, runs through the length of this long, narrow reservation traversing fields and woods. The park is crowded on weekends but nearly empty during the week. Birds provide musical background while deer can often be spotted in the woods.

After the duck pond in about a half mile, the path goes through a parking lot and continues on the other side of a crossroad. Depending on the route you choose at the far end of the parking lot, you may have to veer slightly to the left to pick up the path again. At 8.5 miles, turn right at the bike trail junction; in a short distance you'll pass over a pretty stone bridge. Cross the next road, continuing until you reach the end of the path at Green Village Road. (The Green Village Post Office is just to your right.)

10.4   LEFT on Green Village Road.

Loantaka Brook County Park is delightful to cycle through.

10.8   RIGHT on Hickory Place.
Lovely weeping willows line this street.

11.0   RIGHT on Southern Boulevard.
Pass the sign at the entrance to Great Swamp Outdoor Education Center. The center is a worthwhile stop, but we don't recommend this entrance because of the gravel road.

12.3   RIGHT on Jay Road.
After 0.3 mile, lock your bike to a tree at the cul-de-sac and walk the dirt path that leads to the Outdoor Education Center in about 0.1 mile. This is a good place to take a break, use the rest room, fill your water bottle, and take a stretch over a bit of the two-mile nature trail leading through woods, fields, swamps, and marshes. In addition it has an indoor museum with fine displays of New Jersey wildlife and natural history. When you're ready, pick up your bike and return to Southern Boulevard via Jay Road.

12.9   RIGHT on Southern Boulevard.
This hilly section passes through suburbs.

13.6   RIGHT on Fairmount Avenue.

15.4   RIGHT on Meyersville Road.
There are small hills on this stretch. Woods line the right side of the road.

17.9   RIGHT on New Vernon Road.
You're now entering Meyersville, a good town to buy food and/or drink before reaching the Great Swamp National Wildlife Refuge. Except for the peaceful chirping of birds, the refuge is so extraordinarily quiet that even the gentle rubbing of one tree branch against another can be heard. Only an occasional airplane is a reminder that the refuge is so close to the city and yet far enough away to be a home to abundant wildlife. Large oak and beech trees abound, in addition to laurel, wild orchids, and ferns.
    After leaving the refuge, the road name changes to Long Hill Road, an appropriate name because of the long uphill climb.

21.8   RIGHT at the "T" on Lees Hill Road.

22.2   LEFT at the traffic light on Glen Alpine Road.
This narrow, rutted road without a shoulder is somewhat strenuous.

25.3   RIGHT at the entrance to Jockey Hollow.
Reach starting point at 25.7 miles.

Bicycle shops:
Marty's Reliable Cycle Center, 173 Speedwell Avenue, Morristown, (201) 538-7773.

5

Skylands

Location: Passaic County
Starting point: Ringwood Manor, Ringwood State Park
Terrain: Hilly
Traffic: Light
Round-trip distance pedaled: 22.4 miles
Highlights: Ringwood Manor, Skylands Manor, Skylands Botanical Garden, swimming, boating, fishing.

Cycling the steep hills of the Skylands area is a challenge, but the reward is definitely worth the effort. You'll be pedaling along quiet roads past tall trees, carpets of wildflowers, and beautiful bodies of water. You'll also have an opportunity to explore Ringwood State Park, which includes Ringwood Manor, the state's largest historic site, Skylands Botanical Garden, and Shepherd Lake.

The area was an iron manufacturing center from the 1700s until 1931 when the mines closed. During the Revolutionary War, everything from cannonballs to camp ovens was produced here, including the huge chain placed across the Hudson River to prevent the British from attacking West Point. The same ironworks produced the cannons for "Old Ironsides" and the mortars used by the Union Army during the Civil War.

Park in the main parking lot of the Ringwood Manor section in Ringwood State Park, not far from the Sloatsburg Road entrance. (There is a parking fee from Memorial Day to Labor Day.) Plan on visiting Ringwood Manor, next to the parking lot, before starting out.

The discovery of iron here in 1740 led to the building of a forge and formation of the Ringwood Company. When word of this successful operation reached England, the London Company sent their representative, Peter Hasenclever, to purchase the business and more land. After Hasenclever took over, he opened additional mines, furnaces, and forges and built the original section of Ringwood Manor in 1765.

The business, which was sold a number of times, was finally taken over by Abram S. Hewitt in 1807. In addition to continuing mining operations, Hewitt added many rooms to the mansion, which has served as headquarters for Ringwood Manor State Park since his heirs donated it to the state in 1936.

It is fascinating to explore the inside of the house, which is filled with an eclectic collection of belongings amassed by the owners. Outside the house are a huge Vicksburg mortar, a cannon from "Old Ironsides," and iron-making artifacts. The formal gardens in back of the house are delightful; they contain an assortment of columns, gateposts, a fountain from Versailles, and imported millstones.

When you're ready to begin the bike tour, reset your odometer at the parking lot exit.

0.0   **RIGHT on the main park road, toward the park exit.**

0.2   **STRAIGHT on Sloatsburg Road.**
Traffic along this smooth road is usually light except during summer weekends.

0.9   **RIGHT on Margaret King Avenue.**
This road is quite hilly.

3.2   **LEFT at the "T" on Greenwood Lake Turnpike.**
A newly created reservoir comes into view at 3.5 miles.

3.7   **RIGHT on Stonetown Road.**
You'll come to a panoramic view in 0.3 mile just before beginning a steep climb. The road winds by many new and distinctive houses surrounded by lush woods.

6.8   **RIGHT on Magee Road (at the Ringwood Fire House).**
Houses along this tree-lined, winding road, blend in with the scenery. Look for a tiny cow pasture on your left at 8.0 miles where an old bathtub serves as water trough.

8.1   **LEFT at the "T" on West Brook Road.**
In about a mile follow the road as it bears right, as Stonetown Road joins from the left. At 9.2 miles you'll spot Wanaque Reservoir on the right, and as you continue along this scenic stretch, you'll have panoramic views of its clear blue water.

10.5   **RIGHT at the "T" on Ringwood Avenue.**

10.6   **LEFT on Skyline Lakes Drive.**
Food stores are available if you need supplies.

10.8   **LEFT at the "Y" as the road divides.**
One of the two Skyline lakes is on the right.

11.7   **LEFT on (unmarked) Smokey Ridge Road.**
This is the first left turn after Mountain Glen Road; the grade is extremely steep.

11.9   **RIGHT on (unmarked) Hilltop Road.**
Turn just before the "dead end" sign. Unfortunately, the steep climb continues.

12.0 RIGHT at the "T" on Buena Vista Drive.

Take a deep breath and keep climbing.

12.1 LEFT on Alta Vista Drive.

The road starts steeply uphill, but levels off after a short distance as it curves through an attractive neighborhood and then straightens near the end.

12.9 LEFT on Skyline Drive.

A shopping center is located opposite the road where you turn. Use caution; there's lots of traffic here.

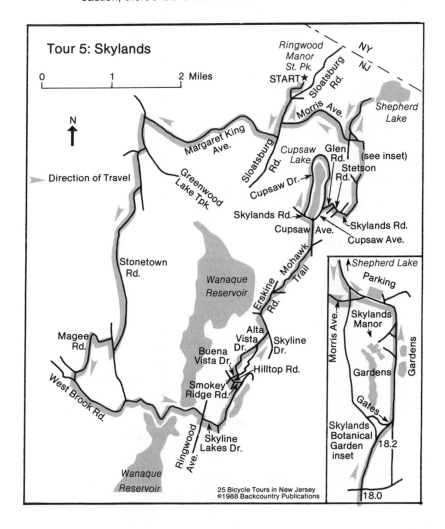

Tour 5: Skylands

25 Bicycle Tours in New Jersey
©1988 Backcountry Publications

13.2   RIGHT on Erskine Road.
You'll be passing a nice sandy beach at Erskine Lake; unfortunately, it's private. You're now on Lakeview Avenue.

14.0   LEFT on Mohawk Trail.

14.4   Bear LEFT on Cupsaw Avenue.
Cross Skylands Road at 14.9 miles, and, if you wish, stop at the market on the left for a cup of coffee, soda, or ice cream.

14.9   LEFT at the "T" at the south end of Cupsaw Lake.

15.0   RIGHT on Cupsaw Drive.
This road follows the lake clockwise past several log cabins, log garages, and houses built with stone foundations and log tops. The houses blend in nicely with the rustic surroundings, and the weeping willows that dip gracefully into the lake add to the pleasant scene. As you travel south along the east side of the lake, you'll have occasional glimpses of boating and swimming activities during summer months.

16.9   Sharp LEFT on Glen Road.
This is a short, but steep, uphill.

17.0   RIGHT on Stetson Road.

17.1   LEFT on Skylands Road.
As you pass through the stone entrance gate into Ringwood State Park in 0.1 mile, you might like to rinse your face with the cool water from the brook that flows under the road.

17.3   RIGHT at the "T" on the unmarked park road.
Follow this paved road as it hooks to the left in a semicircle. Tall trees line both sides of the road leading you to Duck Pond on the left at 17.5 miles. Resembling a Japanese garden, this tranquil spot has large white rocks jutting through the pond's surface and a bench in case you'd like to relax and listen to the birds.

18.0   Bear RIGHT at the "T."

18.2   Bear RIGHT, then LEFT at the "T."
Supported by huge stone pillars, these massive iron gates sport the seal of the state of New Jersey. In 0.1 mile, park and lock your bicycle and walk to the left to explore Skyland Manor and its grounds.
This land, amassed by Francis Lynde Stetson in the mid-1800s from surrounding pioneer farmsteads, was named Skylands Farms. Stetson built an impressive mansion and maintained a working farm, entertaining such friends as Grover Cleveland, Andrew Carnegie, Ethel Barrymore, and J. P. Morgan. When Clarence McKenzie Lewis bought the property in 1922, he immediately set out to make it a

Ringwood Manor, within Ringwood State Park, is an impressive mansion. Take a tour through and see the wealth of items amassed by the many families who lived here and then stroll through the gardens.

botanical showplace, tearing down the Stetson mansion and erecting his own Jacobean mansion of native granite. He collected and planted trees from all over the world as well as from New Jersey roadsides, and today Skylands has one of the finest collections of plants in the state. It was designated the state's official botanic garden in 1984.

When you return to the road, cross to the other side and visit several small gardens. When finished, return to your bicycle, continuing on the same road. The formal annual garden ahead, on the right, has seasonal exhibits. In 0.1 mile, you'll see one of the state's fanciest comfort stations, made of stone. Just after that, as the road swings left, you'll pass a stone pump house.

Take the middle fork when the road divides after passing a parking lot.

18.6 **RIGHT on the road to Shepherd Lake.**

Dense woods line the road; in about 3/4 mile, you will enter a stone and iron gate into the Shepherd Lake section of Ringwood State Park. Turn right to the boating area for a lovely view of the lake. In season, you'll see a number of canoes and sailboats on the lake, and if you have the urge to exercise your arms, rent a canoe or rowboat.

Turn around, and head in the opposite direction toward the swimming area where you'll find rest rooms, a snack bar (in season), and a change house. This is a beautiful place to enjoy a swim. When you're ready to continue, return to the entrance gate and head back on the park road.

20.4 **Bear RIGHT at the stop sign, then RIGHT on Morris Avenue.**

If you glance to your left before turning, you'll see a pair of stone eagles guarding this entrance to the Skylands area.

21.8 **RIGHT on Sloatsburg Road.**

22.1 **Bear LEFT into the Ringwood Manor section of Ringwood State Park.**

You'll arrive at the starting point at 22.4 miles.

6

Bergen's Northwest Corner

Location: Bergen County
Starting point: Bergen County Wildlife Center
Terrain: Moderately hilly
Traffic: Moderate
Round-trip distance pedaled: 21.8 miles
Highlights: Nature centers, bird-watching.

One of the four original counties of New Jersey, Bergen County, created in 1683, is home to nearly one million people, and there are times when it seems as though every one of them is out walking or driving at the same time. However, if you allow enough time to explore the pleasant retreats built into this trip, the more highly travelled areas are tolerable.

The trip begins at the Bergen County Wildlife Center, an excellent place to limber up while enjoying informative exhibits. The center's pond attracts snow geese in the fall, while ducks and turtles are a familiar sight during summer months. Interior exhibits include live frogs, toads, and an enormous Mexican tarantula, as well as samples of various bird eggs and nests. There is also a delightful short trail to explore; you'll pass through an upland forest, streams, and a swamp area. The 81-acre Wildlife Center is open daily 9 a.m. to 5 p.m., except on holidays. There is no admission charge. For further information call (201) 891-5571.

Follow the one-way road out of the parking lot and reset your odometer when you reach the exit.

0.0 RIGHT turn at the parking lot exit on Crescent Avenue.

0.3 RIGHT on Franklin Avenue (Route 502).

The exciting downhill portion is worth the heavy auto traffic along this section.

0.9 LEFT on Crescent Avenue, which turns into West Crescent.

The next few miles take you through the neighborhoods of Waldwick, Allendale, and Ramsey, which are shaded by large trees. On weekends many yard sales are held along this route, so start out with empty saddlebags and lots of change.

2.4 LEFT on Hillside Avenue.

3.8   LEFT on East Oak Street, which becomes West Oak after it crosses Wyckoff Avenue.

4.5   RIGHT on Fuhrman Avenue.

4.9   RIGHT at the "T" on Woodland Avenue.

5.0   LEFT on Jean Street.

5.4   LEFT at the "T" on Darlington Avenue.
          Entering Mahwah you'll pass Darlington County Park, which is popular with fishermen.

7.3   LEFT on Campgaw Road.
          This road should be renamed "Huff and Puff Road" because of the long, steep grade that seems to head straight for the sky. With very little traffic, and a large cemetery to the left, you may feel a bit lonely along this stretch. At the crest of the hill, the Campgaw Mountain County Reservation is a welcome sight.
          The reservation is a good place to rest and have a drink. You may wish to come back some other time to ski or hike on one of the many trails within the park.

10.2 RIGHT at the "T" on Pulis Avenue.
          The pond about half a mile down this road makes a perfect setting for sitting, munching a sandwich, or watching the ducks.

11.7 RIGHT at the "T" on Franklin Avenue.

11.9 LEFT on Colonial Road.
          You are now heading into the luxurious Franklin Lakes area, which has many interesting houses set on large plots of land. The overall feeling is one of spaciousness and gentility.

14.1 LEFT on Lake Drive.
          A pretty lake comes into view after less than half a mile. The road name changes to Dogwood Trail as it meanders along.

14.7 RIGHT on Pueblo Drive.

15.1 RIGHT on High Mountain Road.
          Beautiful large houses line this street. Watch out for fast auto traffic at the circle in about one-half mile. Continue straight ahead.

16.6 LEFT on Ewing Avenue.
          Haledon Reservoir, on the right, can be seen through the trees. The Lorrimer Nature Center, run by the New Jersey Audubon Society, is about nine-tenths of a mile down the road. This is a great place to take a break, fill the canteen, and explore.
          The Visitor Center, built in the 1850s by Lucine L. Lorrimer, houses

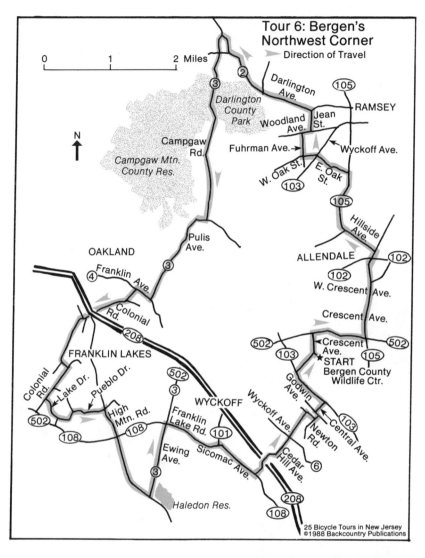

Tour 6: Bergen's Northwest Corner

Direction of Travel

0   1   2 Miles

N

Darlington Ave.

Darlington County Park

105

RAMSEY

Woodland Ave.

Jean St.

Campgaw Rd.

Fuhrman Ave.

Wyckoff Ave.

Campgaw Mtn. County Res.

W. Oak St.

E. Oak St.

103

105

Pulis Ave.

Hillside Ave.

OAKLAND

Franklin Ave.

ALLENDALE

102

4

102

W. Crescent Ave.

Colonial Rd.

Crescent Ave.

208

502

103

Crescent Ave.

502

FRANKLIN LAKES

105

Colonial Rd.

Lake Dr.

Pueblo Dr.

502

START
Bergen County
Wildlife Ctr.

3

Godwin Ave.

High Mtn. Rd.

WYCKOFF

Wyckoff Ave.

502

Franklin Lake Rd.

101

108

108

Newton Rd.

103

Central Ave.

Ewing Ave.

Sicomac Ave.

Cedar Hill Ave.

6

3

208

Haledon Res.

108

25 Bicycle Tours in New Jersey
©1988 Backcountry Publications

a classroom, an observatory, museum, bookshop, and gift shop. Peer through the telescope and you'll probably see a red-tailed hawk, a cardinal, or a devious squirrel trying to steal the seed from the bird feeders. A self-guided trail system meanders through the field and woodland where deer, raccoons, and rabbits are frequently spotted. Trails are open daily from dawn until dusk; the Visitor Center and rest room are open Tuesday through Saturday from 10 a.m. to 4 p.m. and

Sunday from 1 to 5 p.m. There is no admission charge. For further information call (201) 891-1211.

If you stop to visit the sanctuary, return to the Ewing Avenue entrance when you are ready to continue and turn LEFT, heading north.

17.6   RIGHT on Franklin Lake Road, which becomes Sicomac Avenue.

19.3   LEFT on Cedar Hill Avenue.

Stay left (toward Oakland) at the Oakland and Fairlawn sign and follow the road across the highway. Use extreme caution here; watch out for fast automobile traffic.

A closer look at Canada geese at the Bergen County Wildlife Center.

20.6   LEFT on Newton Road; then make the first LEFT followed by the first RIGHT onto Central Avenue.

20.8   LEFT on Godwin Avenue.

21.4   RIGHT at the sign for the Bergen County Wildlife Center on Crescent Avenue.

Arrive at the Wildlife Center, the end of the trip, at 21.8 miles.

Bicycle shops:
There are none along this route.

7

South Mountain

Location: Essex County
Starting point: Center for Environmental Studies
Terrain: Very hilly
Traffic: Moderate
Round-trip distance pedaled: 26.1 miles
Highlights: Center for Environmental Studies exhibition, glacial moraine, fishing, beautiful scenery in the South Mountain Reservation, arts and crafts studios.

If Robert Treat were still alive he could probably sell the Brooklyn Bridge. Back in 1666, after leaving Connecticut with a group of Puritans to establish a new community in New Jersey, Treat purchased most of what is now Essex and Union counties from the Lenni-Lenape Indians for a mere "50 double hands of powder, 100 bars of lead, 20 axes, 20 coats, 10 guns, 20 pistols, 10 breeches, 50 knives, 20 hoes, 850 fathoms of wampum, three troopers coats, and 32 gallons of water." The Indians must have been pleased, because 11 years later, they sold the settlers more land, including the top of what is now South Mountain, for only "two guns, three coats, and some rum."

Essex County has changed through the years from lovely meadows and lush woodland to one of the most densely populated and industrialized counties in the state. However, it boasts the oldest county park system in the country and has over 5,000 acres of parks, reservations, and golf courses.

If you don't know what shape you're in, cycling up and down the hills of western Essex County is an excellent test. To avoid rush-hour traffic, plan on coming on a weekend, but start out early in the morning to beat shopping-mall traffic.

Begin at the Center for Environmental Studies at 621 Eagle Rock Avenue within West Essex Park. If this parking lot is filled, continue to Mohawk Lane, adjacent to the center. Plan on spending a little time inside the center; it has exhibits ranging from dinosaur footprints found a mile away to a chart of edible mushrooms that grow in nearby parks. You can also limber up on a short trail in back and pick up a free schedule of upcoming canoe trips, hikes, or bird-watching sessions that the center runs. (Open 9 a.m. to 4:30 p.m., except on major holidays; there is no admission charge.)

Reset your odometer as you exit the parking lot.

0.0   RIGHT (east) on Eagle Rock Avenue.

Traffic is sometimes heavy along this four-lane, mostly uphill stretch

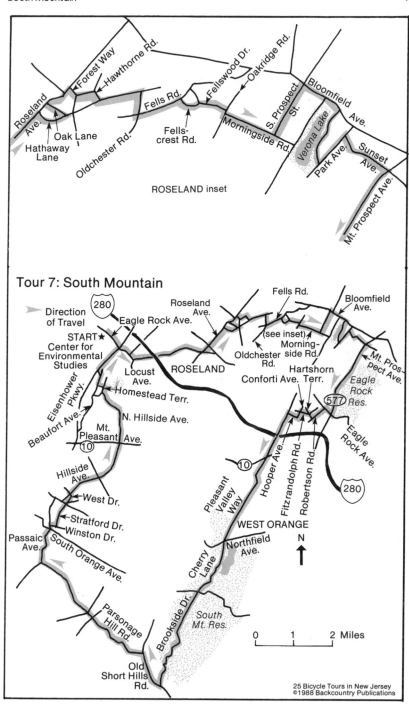

ROSELAND inset

Tour 7: South Mountain

25 Bicycle Tours in New Jersey
©1988 Backcountry Publications

through the Borough of Roseland. If you turn off to the right at Locust Avenue, you'll see the remains of the Riker Hill Quarry carved from a section of mountain. Fossilized dinosaur footprints were discovered here in 1971. You'll also see a pile of rocky debris formed about 15,000 years ago when this area was covered by the Wisconsin glacier. As the glacier receded, rocks and sand were deposited, and the smooth stones now suspended in fine soil are typical of what is called a moraine.

2.3   LEFT on Roseland Avenue.
In the mid-1700s, stage coaches struggled along this same road, fighting rocks, ruts, and dust.

2.9   RIGHT on Hathaway Lane.
Numerous turn-of-the-century mansions are along this uphill stretch. Of particular interest is the Lafayette Ryerson House at 79 Hathaway Lane. Originally constructed in 1787 and moved from Wayne, New Jersey, to this location, it is built on eleven different levels, has six fireplaces, and is said to have contained slave quarters.

3.2   LEFT on Oak Lane at the "Do Not Enter" sign.

3.4   RIGHT on Roseland Avenue.
On the left are Tudor-style St. Peter's Episcopal Church and the stylish Essex Fells municipal offices.

3.5   RIGHT on Forest Way; then LEFT on Hawthorne Road.
Ride between the stone pillars and go past the school. As you pedal to the top of the hill, you'll have time to admire the thick stands of rhododendron growing on both sides of the road. During springtime, the blossoms put on a dazzling show.

4.2   RIGHT on Oldchester Road.
No doubt your calves are beginning to feel the continuing pressure of the uphill climb. More is coming!

4.4   LEFT at the stop sign on Fells Road.

4.7   RIGHT on Fellscrest Road.
This is a very steep hill, but there are many attractive houses to admire while shifting gears.

4.9   RIGHT at the "T" on Fellswood Drive.
At long last, the road decends – steeply.

5.2   RIGHT at the "T" on (unmarked) Oakridge Road, then LEFT at the first intersection, Morningside Road.
Continuing downhill, you'll enter Verona.

5.7 LEFT on South Prospect Street.

6.3 RIGHT on Bloomfield Avenue.

This street has many stores, food shops, and restaurants. The attractive building on the left with a clock and cupola is Verona's Municipal Building and to the right is Vernona Park. After all the uphill work, you may want to take a break near the lovely lake and admire the weeping willow trees. You can also spend some time fishing or rent a boat. If you come during winter, bring a pair of ice skates along.

6.6 RIGHT on the entrance road into Verona Park (at the sign).

7.0 LEFT at the "T" on Park Avenue.

7.2 RIGHT on Sunset Avenue.

Start uphill for 0.1 mile, passing the Montclair Golf Club on the right.

7.7 RIGHT on Mount Prospect Avenue.

This starts out steeply but levels after 0.3 mile, followed by many ups and downs. Traffic may be heavy. At about 8.3 miles, you'll come to Eagle Rock Reservation, named after the craggy cliffs once frequented by eagles. You'll know you've entered West Orange Township when you see the opulent Manor Restaurant on the right. There

Riker Hill Art Park, a converted Nike tracking station, has artist's studios and outdoor sculpture.

is usually a lot of congestion at the large shopping center at about 9.1 miles, and the going can be slow for a few minutes.

9.3   RIGHT on Eagle Rock Avenue.

9.5   LEFT on Robertson Road.

9.8   RIGHT at the "T" on Hartshorn Terrace.

9.9   LEFT on Fitzrandolph Road.
This road goes downhill sharply.

10.0   LEFT on Conforti Avenue.

10.2   RIGHT at the "T" on Hooper Avenue.
Houses along this stretch are very attractive.

10.4   LEFT on Pleasant Valley Way.
This four-lane road has lots of traffic. Be aware of grates along the curb. At 11.1 miles, there are a few stores, a gas station, and a golf course as you cross Route 10.

13.0   STRAIGHT across Northfield Avenue onto Cherry Lane.
You are now in the South Mountain Reservation. Covering 2,048 acres, it is the largest of the county's reservations. Within the park lie the First and Second Watchung mountains, Hemlock Falls, the west branch of the Rahway River, and a wide variety of flora and fauna.

After entering, you'll pass by a reservoir, lush stands of trees, fields, picnic, and play areas. There are many quiet spots to take a break or eat lunch along this hilly road. The numerous curves will keep you awake should the scenery prove too tranquil. Just before coming to Glen Avenue, the park's southern boundary, you'll pass a pond at 15.9 miles.

Continue straight ahead as the road name changes to Brookside Drive, going past the Paper Mill Playhouse. Built around 1800, the playhouse was operated as a paper mill until after World War I. Today it is one of the most acclaimed theaters in New Jersey.

16.3   RIGHT on Old Short Hills Road.
As you enter Millburn Township, named for the many paper mills that once flourished in the area and the "burn," the Scots word for stream, the road climbs for a short stretch past large, beautiful houses.

17.1   LEFT on Parsonage Hill Road.
There's lots of foliage along this curving, hilly (mostly uphill), wide, lightly used road. Another park comes into view at 18.3 miles, just before a Presbyterian church, founded in 1831, on the right. Deer are frequently spotted in the wooded area ahead.

19.8 **RIGHT on Passaic Avenue.**

This wide, single-lane street is usually busy with traffic. At 20.5 miles, there is a large shopping center in case you need supplies. Continue straight ahead to the first street past South Orange Avenue, which is a major intersection.

20.6 **RIGHT on Winston Drive, then LEFT on Stratford Drive.**

As you make the turn, glance over to the right to see an unusual all-white, Spanish-style house. It's one of many styles found in this section.

21.2 **Bear LEFT at the "Y" onto West Drive.**

21.4 **RIGHT at the stop sign on (unmarked) Hillside Avenue.**

True to its name, you'll climb uphill here as the road winds. There are small, alpine-style houses on the left at 21.9 miles. (West Essex Hospital is straight ahead if the hills have proven too much for you.) Otherwise, continue on as the road name changes to North Hillside just after it crosses Mt. Pleasant Drive. At 23.7 miles, there is a crest affording a view to the west.

24.0 **RIGHT on Homestead Terrace, then an immediate RIGHT.**

Riker Hill Art Park is about 0.1 mile ahead. This area, once a Nike tracking station, has been converted to studios for artists and craftspeople. If you take the left fork, you'll come to the potters' studios. It's a good place to stop and chat for a few minutes; the artists are friendly and willing to explain what they're doing. There is also a geological museum here, open weekdays only. When you're ready to move on, leave on the same road you entered on. Then continue straight ahead, past Homestead Terrace.

24.6 **RIGHT at the "T" on Beaufort Avenue.**

24.9 **LEFT at the end of the street; then RIGHT on Eisenhower Parkway.**

25.6 **LEFT on Eagle Rock Avenue.**

Arrive at the starting point at 26.1 miles.

8
Old Tappan

Location: Bergen County
Starting point: Benjamin Franklin Junior High School, Teaneck
Terrain: Mostly flat
Traffic: Light to moderate
Round-trip distance pedaled: 23.7 miles
Highlights: Historic churches, gravestone rubbing, interesting architecture, fishing.

Where there's a will, there definitely is a way, and our friends Laura and Marvin Mausner found it. After deciding that having young children wouldn't stop them from enjoying their bicycling, they had only one problem: rear bicycle seats for children weren't around thirty years ago! Luckily, Marvin was ingenious; he simply cut the legs off his kitchen chairs, fastened the seats to the back fender, and off they rode. When the children grew too heavy, Marvin came up with a solution once again; he got them their own bikes.

Laura and Marvin shared these memories with us, inviting us to join them on the same route through Bergen County they rode with their children thirty years ago. Amazingly, Marvin is still riding the same three-speed bicycle that carried his son and took him on trips throughout the United States and parts of Europe.

Bergen County, located in the northeastern corner of New Jersey, has a rich past. Created in 1683, Bergen is one of the four original counties of New Jersey; its first settlers were chiefly Dutch along with some French Huguenots. Because of its strategic location on the Hudson River and its proximity to New York City, Bergen County played an important role during the Revolutionary War.

Along the route, you will pass old churches, several small parks, and fine examples of Dutch red sandstone houses. Come on a weekend not only to avoid rush-hour traffic but for an opportunity to pick up inexpensive merchandise at one of the many garage sales along the route.

Park at the parking lot of Benjamin Franklin Junior High School on Windsor Road, just north of the Route 4 overpass. Set your odometer to 0.0 at the parking lot exit.

0.0   LEFT (north) on Windsor Road onto the bike lane.

This is a quiet residential section and leads past Windsor Park at 0.2 mile. We took this trip during early morning hours on a hot, humid,

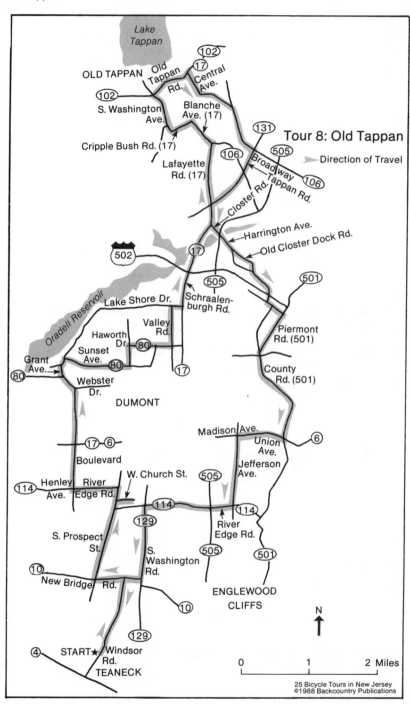

25 Bicycle Tours in New Jersey
©1988 Backcountry Publications

summer day and enjoyed the shade provided by large trees on the side of the road.

1.1   **LEFT (west) at the traffic light on New Bridge Road.**
Veterans Memorial Park, which has tennis courts and other facilities open to the public, is on the right.

1.5   **RIGHT (north) on South Prospect (at sign for Dumont).**

2.6   **RIGHT on West Church Street.**
Old South Church, on the left, was organized in 1723 as the Schraalenburgh Dutch Reform Church; the original building was erected in 1728 just 150 feet to the east of its present location. The church became Presbyterian in 1913. Many Revolutionary War soldiers are buried in the churchyard.

A bit farther up the street is Cooper's Pond, a lovely small park with a duck pond. Here you can take a break in the shade of the pagoda; watch the ducks, seagulls, and geese; and admire the lovely spring, summer, and fall flowers. The park path takes only a few minutes to cycle.

3.0   **RIGHT on West Church Street. Return to Prospect Avenue and make a RIGHT turn, continuing north.**

3.2   **LEFT on River Edge Road, which changes to Henley Avenue.**
This street goes uphill for a short distance.

4.0   **RIGHT on Boulevard.**
Follow Boulevard as it swings to the left at 4.5 miles, with Webster Drive coming in on the right. The road name then changes to Grant Avenue.

5.1   **RIGHT on Sunset Avenue, following signs to Dumont.**
The Oradell Reservoir is on your left as you turn. If you're interested in fishing or stopping for a snack along the reservoir, take Lake Shore Drive (go straight ahead instead of turning right) for a short distance as it follows the edge of the reservoir.

Sunset Avenue has many large, lovely houses and an expansive country club.

6.1   **LEFT at sign for County Route 80 (Haworth Drive).**

6.4   **RIGHT, still following Route 80.**
Some of the houses here are in Tudor style with stone facades. After about 0.5 mile along this road, you'll come to a park with a small duck pond and benches.

7.1   **LEFT at the traffic light onto Valley Road.**

7.6   RIGHT at the "T," then an immediate LEFT at the traffic light on Schraalenburgh Road (County Route 17).

After 0.9 mile, cross the bridge over the Oradell Reservoir.

8.9   Bear LEFT as Closter Road comes in from the right.

Stay on Route 17, which changes names and directions several times as it winds through wooded and residential areas. At 10.0 miles, you'll come to Pond Side Park, about half way along the route and a good spot for lunch. Approaching the center of the town of Old Tappan, you'll be on South Washington Avenue.

11.3   RIGHT on Old Tappan Road.

As soon as you turn, you'll see the Old Tappan Sunday School, a fine example of vernacular stick-style architecture. Founded in 1883, it was the first ecclesiastical building in Old Tappan and the only place of worship in town until the 1950s. Continuing through the town, which was settled in 1682, you'll pass Trinity Reformed Church and several municipal buildings.

11.8   RIGHT on Central Avenue.

If you need supplies, there's a shopping center to your left. After you pass the mall, you'll see local schools and several wooded areas.

13.4   RIGHT on Tappan Road.

After approximately 0.3 mile, at the corner of Blanche Avenue, slow down for a look at the Campbell-Blanche House to your left. This stone house is believed to have been erected around 1790. The "Old Burying Ground" is 0.7 mile farther down the road and worth a look. Stairs and handrails have been built into the hillside as an aid in reaching the site, which is hidden from view. Over 40 stones with single or multiple arches can be seen here; the burial ground, known

Cooper's Pond, a lovely small park with a duck pond, is a good place to rest.

as the Blauvelt Cemetery, has historical significance since it contains the graves of early settlers in Harrington Park who fought in the American Revolution; the earliest burial dates from 1722.

14.5 LEFT on County Route 17 South.

14.6 LEFT onto Closter Road.

This is not a sharp turn. The main road (Route 17) swings to the right as you bear left heading for the center of Closter. Two cycle shops are on the left side. The street name has become Harrington Avenue and soon changes to Old Closter Dock Road. Stick with it as it turns sharply to the left at 16.0 miles.

16.3 RIGHT on Piermont Road at the traffic light.

This is County Route 501. Stay on this road; as it twists along its name changes to County Road. Canada geese flock at the small local park on the right at 17.1 miles.

18.3 RIGHT on Union Avenue.

A few blocks south of this corner is Huyler's Landing Road. During colonial times, a crude road connected this area with the Hudson River. Cornwallis used it to attack Fort Lee in 1776, and it was also useful to the Tories when they travelled it in 1779 to raid local houses. After George Huyler improved the road in 1840, it became a major route for farm produce transported to New York until the railroad was built in 1859.

Union Avenue changes to Madison Avenue. Cross the railroad tracks.

18.9 LEFT on Jefferson Avenue at the traffic light.

After 0.7 mile, you'll see the Christie-Parsels House at 195 Jefferson Avenue, another good example of an early stone house with a gabled roof. One wing of this house dates to 1804 and the main structure to 1836. It stands on land purchased by William Christie for five pounds sterling per acre.

20.0 RIGHT on River Edge Road.

21.3 LEFT on South Washington Avenue.

22.3 RIGHT on New Bridge Road.

22.6 LEFT on Windsor Road.

23.7 Arrive at final destination: school parking lot.

Bicycle shops:
Amber Cyclery, 764 Palisade Avenue, Teaneck, (201) 836-0104.
All-County Schwinn Cyclery, 237 Closter Dock Road, Closter Dock, (201) 768-3086.

Central New Jersey

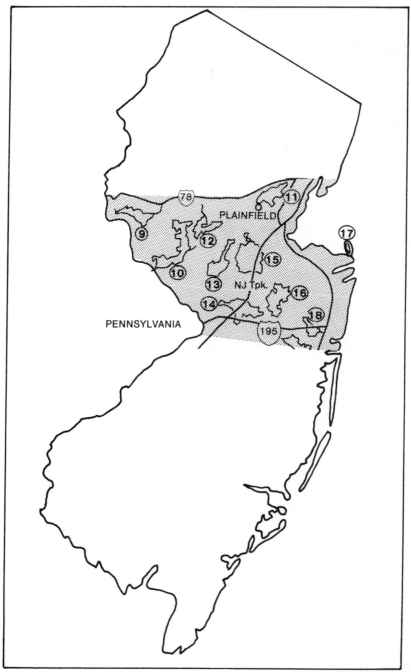

9

Clinton

Location: Hunterdon County
Starting point: A & P Parking Lot, Route 173, Clinton
Terrain: Hilly
Traffic: Light
Round-trip distance pedaled: 40.3 miles
Highlights: Clinton Historical Museum Village, Volendam Windmill, historic build-
ings, country scenery, gravestone rubbing.

Clinton, a peaceful, picturesque eighteenth-century village, is the perfect
starting point for this excursion into the hills of northwest Hunterdon. Plan on
arriving early in the morning to explore the Clinton Historical Museum Village,
the Hunterdon Art Center, and an authenic model of a wind-driven mill. While
this trip is somewhat strenuous, you'll be rewarded by dramatic panoramic
vistas of well-kept farms and woods and attractive houses inhabited by
people who shun city crowds. Many crisscrossing roads may be taken to
shorten the trip, if you wish.

Park at the A & P shopping center on Old Route 22 (now Route 173) in
Clinton. Take the parking lot exit opposite the Clinton Rescue Squad, resetting your odometer at the street junction.

0.0   RIGHT on Old Route 22.

0.4   RIGHT on Main Street.

The entrance to the Clinton Historical Museum Village is at 0.1 mile.
Here, nestled between vertical limestone cliffs and the South Branch
of the Raritan River, stands a mill built around 1763 by David McKin-
ney. First used to grind flax seeds to make linseed oil, the mill
changed hands several times before finally passing to the Hunt family.
People flocked to the area after the mill was built, and the town that
sprung up was named, appropriately enough, Hunt's Mills. Later, to
honor Governor DeWitt Clinton of New York, the town's name was
changed to Clinton.

The mill started as a gristmill and later was used for grinding talc
and making graphite until it stopped production completely. Today,
four floors of the mill are open to the public for self-guided tours. Here,
you can see the mechanisms of a gristmill and examine an impressive
eighteenth-century kitchen, a fascinating display of early lighting de-
vices, a harness shop, plus much more. (The Museum Village is open

Tuesday through Sunday, 10 a.m. to 5 p.m., from April to October. There is an admission charge.)

When finished, return to Main Street.

0.5   **RIGHT across the bridge over the South Branch of the Raritan River.**

0.6   **LEFT on Lower Center Street.**
This is the first possible left turn after crossing the bridge. The Hunterdon Art Center, housed in a large stone building on your left just after making the turn, features changing exhibits and is worth a stop. (Hours are Tuesday through Friday, 12 noon to 4:30 p.m., and Saturday and Sunday, 1 to 5 p.m. Donations are requested.) You may wish to walk through the center of town before continuing on Lower Center Street. The downtown area has many ornate Victorian and Greek Revival houses as well as public buildings, looking much the same as they did a century ago.

0.7   **RIGHT on Leigh Street.**
This pretty street, which becomes Hamden Road after leaving Clinton, has several small hills.

2.3   **RIGHT at the unmarked intersection on Hamden Road.**
This turn, easy to miss, comes after Kent Court and continues on an older road that used to be the main drag before new housing developments were built. Cross the narrow steel bridge over the South Branch at 2.5 miles.

2.8   **RIGHT on Lower Landsdown Road.**

3.2   **LEFT on Landsdown Road.**
Tall trees shading this narrow road provide camouflage for birds, which nevertheless make their presence known by their loud chirping.

4.0   **LEFT on Sidney Road and RIGHT on Lower Kingtown Road.**
Cross Capoolong Creek, which parallels the road a couple of times. This is a fairly steep but short uphill section. The stone house and red barns you'll pass blend in nicely with their surroundings.

5.5   **LEFT on Pittstown Road, Route 513.**
Pittstown was a natural choice for settlers because its location along the Capoolong Creek made it an ideal location for building a dam and mill. In less than a mile you'll be able to purchase food and drink and recover from the uphill stretch.

6.5   **STRAIGHT on Route 579.**

6.8   **STRAIGHT on Route 615.**
After a pond, you'll come to a scenic valley and orchards where, in season, you can purchase apple cider.

8.3   RIGHT on Baker Road.

No wonder the grass looks so perfect; you're passing a sod farm!

9.5   RIGHT at the "T" on unmarked Oak Summit Road.

9.8   LEFT on Senator Stout Road.

So many cornfields crop up in this area that some cyclists might call this a "corny" trip.

11.1   STRAIGHT on Route 519 north.

The panoramic views of the surrounding countryside are marvelous here as you dip up and down the hills. In a couple of miles, there is an opportunity to purchase food and drink. Afterward, watch for a large cemetery on the right. Built in the 1700s and used by an English Presbyterian congregation, it was later shared by German settlers. Together, both congregations erected a new church in 1802 that is still in use today. If you enjoy gravestone rubbing, this is the place to try.

14.1   STRAIGHT on Route 631.

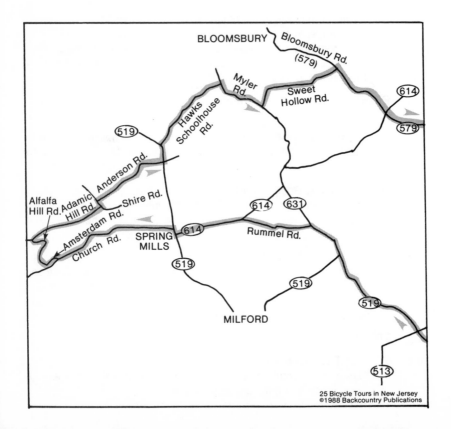

25 Bicycle Tours in New Jersey
©1988 Backcountry Publications

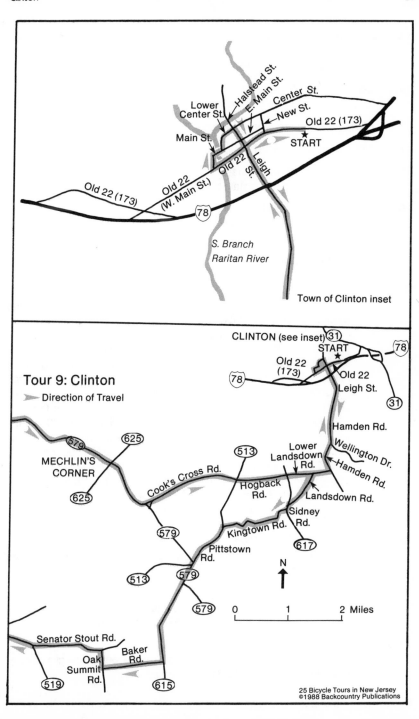

Town of Clinton inset

Tour 9: Clinton

Direction of Travel

CLINTON (see inset)

25 Bicycle Tours in New Jersey
©1988 Backcountry Publications

14.9 **LEFT on Rummel Road.**
This exceptionally beautiful, hilly stretch of road through Holland Township, offers breathtaking views off to the right.

16.1 **Bear LEFT on Route 614, toward Spring Mills.**
This section has some of the most attractive farms along this route.

17.4 **RIGHT at the stop sign on Route 519.**

17.5 **LEFT on Church Road.**

19.9 **RIGHT on Amsterdam Road.**
The goldfinches, the state bird of New Jersey, seem to favor this spot.

20.1 **RIGHT on Alfalfa Hill Road.**
Wisely named and heavily endowed with trees, this road begins a steep half-mile climb.

20.9 **RIGHT on Adamic Hill Road.**
It's easy to think you're in Holland when arriving at the Volendam Windmill Museum, less than a mile up the road on your left. Lock your bicycle to the fence or a tree, eat lunch atop the hill adjoining the windmill, and take a short tour of the windmill designed and built by Poul Jorgensen and his wife, May, in 1965 Named after the town of Volendam in the northern part of the Netherlands, near Amsterdam, the museum demonstrates how a wind-driven mill is used for grinding raw grain into flour. The arms, capable of producing 40 horsepower, are sufficient to turn the one-ton millstone within the 60-foot-high mill. Inside, you can examine old milling tools, huge gears made of applewood, wooden shoes, farm implements, and the mill's 68-foot tip-to-tip sail arms at close range. (The windmill is open weekends May through September from noon to 5 p.m., but if you call (201) 955-4365 and say you're coming, Ms. Jorgensen may open it for you. There is an admission charge.) A clean outhouse is on the grounds. Continue on Adamic Hill Road when finished.

22.4 **LEFT on Shire Road.**

22.5 **RIGHT on Anderson Road.**
Beautiful blue spruces, mimosas, weeping willows, and maples adorn the local houses.

24.1 **LEFT at the "T" on Route 519.**
Prepare for a steep uphill climb for a short distance. Rest rooms and a soda machine are available at a gas station ahead.

24.5 **RIGHT on Hawks Schoolhouse Road.**
Hold on tight; the road is rough for a while but offers glimpses of beautiful views, open fields, and farms.

26.1   RIGHT at the "T" on unmarked Myler Road.

To make up for all the climbs, there is a long downhill stretch, which is steep in spots. It begins to level off just before the road ends.

27.1   LEFT at the "T" on Sweet Hollow Road.

Despite the houses, there is a feeling of solitude here among the tall trees. Now you have to pay the price for coasting down Myler Road; this is mostly uphill, getting steeper as you go. Keep an eye open about a mile up the road, on the left, for a tree trunk that has been carved out to resemble an old man with a beard.

The mill at Clinton Historical Museum Village.

28.8   **RIGHT at the "T" on Route 579.**

Hardly any traffic mars the beautiful views along this stretch of road. In less than a mile you'll begin a steep descent, but the breeze whistling through your helmet is short-lived because the next hill is within sight.

You'll pass a vineyard, apple orchards, acres and acres of corn, and a "pick-your-own" raspberry patch (in season). Spruce Run Reservoir is to the left at 32.3 miles, and at 33.2 miles you'll come to Mechling's Corner Tavern, built in 1752. The most popular drink in the Tavern was probably Hunterdon apple brandy made from home-grown apples, since every land owner in the area during the nineteenth century was required to plant one apple tree for each acre of owned land. After this, you'll pass through more woods and cornfields.

34.2   **LEFT on Cook's Cross Road.**

There is no shoulder on this bumpy road. Usually farmers can be seen working in these fields. The road name changes to Hogback Road and then to Lower Landsdown Road. You'll cross a beautiful one-lane bridge at 37.4 miles.

38.0   **LEFT on Hamden Road.**

38.5   **LEFT at the "T" on unmarked Hamden Road.**

40.0   **RIGHT on Route 173 in Clinton.**

Arrive at the starting point at 40.3 miles.

10

Flemington and Lambertville

Location: Hunterdon County
Starting point: Deer Path Park
Terrain: Hilly with a few steep climbs
Traffic: Light
Round-trip distance pedaled: 75.3 miles
Highlights: Historic buildings, outlet stores and antique shops, magnificent rural scenery, Delaware River, Delaware Canal.

Hunterdon County, in the west central part of the state, is steeped in history and blessed with deep valleys, gentle hills, sparkling rivers, dense woods, and pastoral scenery. It is one of New Jersey's leading agricultural counties, and the route goes past many dairy and horse farms as well as numerous historic sites in towns and villages dating back to pre-Revolutionary days.

This two-day tour begins a short distance from Flemington, which has served as the county seat since 1791 and which is one of the largest outlet centers in the state. Flemington gained national fame in 1935 when Bruno Richard Hauptmann was tried in this courthouse and found guilty of kidnapping and murdering the Lindbergh baby. The courthouse is still here, as are many of the interesting Victorian structures.

Although housing developments are springing up throughout Hunterdon County, the countryside still provides one tranquil scene after another with cows and horses grazing lazily in the fields alongside roads relatively free of traffic.

New Hope, Pennsylvania, once described by William Penn as "the most beautiful of landscapes," is along this route. The tour affords a glimpse of revolutionary-era cottages, artists' workshops, tiny gardens, and an opportunity to ride a mule-drawn barge that carried coal along the canal over 150 years ago.

Plan on staying overnight at Lambertville or at New Hope, just across the Delaware River. (Write to South Hunterdon Chamber of Commerce, 4 South Union Street, Lambertville, N.J. 08530 or the Bucks County Tourist Commission, 152 Swamp Road, Doylestown, Pa. 18901 for information on hotels and motels. Some accommodations require a two-day minimum stay on weekends.)

Begin at Deer Path Park on West Woodschurch Road off Route 31, north of Flemington. Fishing and picnicking are popular activities in the park, and swimming is available at the YMCA located on the grounds. (The pool is open daily from 8 a.m. to 4:30 p.m.; there is an admission fee.) A parking lot is located outside the YMCA; another one is at the end of the paved road.

Reset your odometer to 0.0 at the exit from the park at the junction with West Woodschurch Road.

0.0   RIGHT on West Woodschurch Road.
Many gradual and steep climbs lie ahead after a delightful 0.4-mile downhill stretch, but the extra effort is definitely worth the perspiration. The slightly choppy road passes picturesque farms and newly built houses.

0.7   RIGHT at the "T" as Woodschurch Road joins in from the left.
Sprawling farms and open fields abound in this area.

1.2   RIGHT at the "T" on (unmarked) Route 523.

1.8   LEFT on Barley Sheaf Road.
If the pleasant curves along this road don't keep you awake, its choppy surface will!

2.5   RIGHT on Rockafellows Mill Road.
The road is very narrow and bumpy, but the interesting farms, silos, and open fields make up for the discomfort. Just before the road's end, a small bridge takes you across the South Branch; enjoy this beautiful spot.

4.5   RIGHT at the "T" on (unmarked) River Road.
Canada geese and mallards can usually be seen along the banks of the South Branch of the Raritan River.

4.8   RIGHT at the first road junction, continuing on River Road.
As you pedal through this area, the scenic side of the road is immediately evident. The calm river, flanked by lush farms, flows to the right, while chemical and plastic companies mar the view to the left.

5.7   LEFT (south) on Route 523.
After crossing State Route 31, you'll enter East Main Street in Flemington. An attractive Presbyterian church, built in 1791, stands opposite an impressive stone-arched gate with ornate wrought iron adornments.

7.1   RIGHT at the traffic circle on Pennsylvania Avenue; then an immediate LEFT on Main Street.
A Civil War memorial, complete with cannon, occupies the center of this circle. Main Street, usually congested with shoppers on weekends, has a number of outlet stores and restaurants. You may wish to stop, browse, and perhaps fill your saddle bags with bargains. In any case, examine a few of the historic buildings along this street.

Cyclists are welcome inside the large Union Hotel, built in 1772.

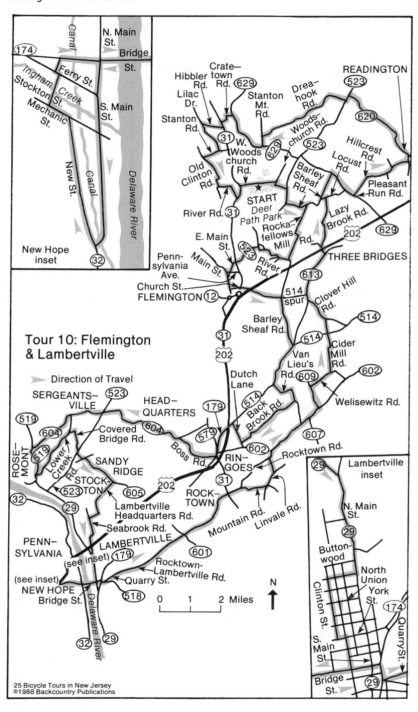

Tour 10: Flemington
& Lambertville

Direction of Travel

Have a drink or lunch, explore its handsome interior, and feel free to use the rest room facilities. The Chamber of Commerce, located in the same building, has free brochures listing nearby attractions. Opposite the hotel is the Greek Revival courthouse, built in 1828, which gained worldwide attention during the trial of Bruno Hauptman. The Doric House, at 114 Main Street, sports fine exterior woodcarving; built in 1846, it is now the headquarters of the Hunterdon County Historical Society and is open for tours, by appointment. Next to it is a handsome Methodist church, built of stone.

7.7   LEFT on Church Street.
The Ponderosa restaurant at 8.0 miles has an excellent soup and salad bar in addition to soft drinks, ice cream, and rest rooms.

After crossing U.S. Highway 202, traffic thins as the road widens and passes housing developments and farms.

9.5   RIGHT on Barley Sheaf Road.
This turn takes you into a peaceful rural area.

11.3   RIGHT at the "T" on Route 514 West following the sign for Ringoes.

12.7   LEFT on Van Lieu's Road.
Corn sways in the breeze and, in season, you'll pass places where you can hand-pick strawberries.

13.8   RIGHT on Back Brook Road (just before the one-lane bridge).
New houses are springing up along this narrow road.

16.1   RIGHT at the "T" on Dutch Lane.
This stretch begins with a short uphill climb, but stick with it; there'll be a breeze as you pedal downhill.

16.8   LEFT at the "T" on Old York Road (Route 514).
Use caution crossing Routes 202 and 31; you're now on Route 179 as you enter the historic town of Ringoes. The Indians followed this same path as they travelled between the Delaware and Raritan rivers.

18.1   RIGHT on Boss Road.
After about 0.4 mile admire the picture-postcard scene. A large maple tree stands at the perfect spot on the roadside.

19.6   LEFT at the "T" on (unmarked) Route 604.
This smooth road has hardly any traffic. At 22.7 miles, you'll reach shops, a restaurant, and a general store in the village of Headquarters. As you head back into farm country, you'll be going downhill for a change.

When you reach Sergeantsville at 23.8 miles, you'll pass through New Jersey's only covered bridge. There are many theories about why covered bridges were constructed. Some think it was to keep horses from rearing when passing over the water; others think it was to protect the bridge from the elements. The most charming theory is that engineers with romance in their soul built covered bridges to allow young couples a chance to stop their carriage and embrace for a moment in privacy!

After the bridge, the road goes uphill through more exquisite farm scenery.

25.6 LEFT at the "T" on Route 519.
The town of Rosemont has a general store and some antique stores. Follow Route 519 as it turns left at the sign for Stockton. At 26.3 miles you'll begin a steep descent.

26.7 Sharp LEFT onto (unmarked) Lower Creek Road.
After a hairpin turn, you'll practically be going back in the same direction you came from. A dark, cool stretch of forest follows beside a creek on the right. Wildflowers grow profusely along both sides of the narrow road. After climbing steeply uphill and crossing the bridge, the creek will be on your left.

28.7 RIGHT on (unmarked) Covered Bridge Road.
This extremely narrow road starts out steeply uphill.

29.5 RIGHT on Route 523.

29.6 LEFT on Route 605 (south).
Jog to the left, then right, at the "T" at 30.0 miles in Sandy Ridge. Some small hills follow through open country.

31.3 RIGHT on (unmarked) Lambertville Headquarters Road.
As you turn, you'll squeeze past a small, squarish white building very close to the road.

33.0 LEFT at the "T" on Seabrook Road.
Enjoy the downhill cruise.

33.9 LEFT on Route 29 just past the Route 202 overpass.
USE CAUTION: This short stretch along Route 29 north of Lambertville is a four-lane highway with lots of traffic.

Lambertville, settled in 1705, is one of the oldest communities in Hunterdon County. During colonial times, the town thrived. Not only was it a popular stop along the stagecoach route between New York and Pennsylvania, but its thriving industry included a canning factory, brickyard, shoe factory, linen mill, and an ironworks. The town gained a place in history when Washington visited during his campaigns of 1777 and 1778. Today Lambertville is popular for the recreational facilities it offers at the Delaware and Raritan Canal State Park. When the canal opened in 1834, Lambertville was an important stop on the feeder link since barges could carry products from here to Trenton or New Brunswick.

In addition to the historic sites, there are rows of quaint houses built very close to each other during the mid-nineteenth century. They have interesting roofs, turrets, and tiny porches upon which residents view the passersby. Properties are now being restored, and no doubt the town will soon be thriving with a tourist trade.

34.5   RIGHT on Buttonwood Street.

34.7   LEFT on (unmarked) Clinton Street.
This is the last street on which a left turn is possible.

35.0   LEFT on York Street, then RIGHT on North Union Street.
This street, lined with restaurants, art studios, and antique stores, also has a small and interesting Civil War memorial.

35.2   RIGHT at the traffic light on Bridge Street.
Historic Lambertville House, built in 1812 by Senator Lambert, was originally called Lambert's Inn. Continuously hosting weary travellers since its founding, it has served many famous people such as President Andrew Johnson, General Tom Thumb, and General Grant. Next to it is Lambertville Station, consisting of a restaurant, inn, and antique shops.

The boyhood home of James Wilson Marshall is at 60 Bridge Street. When Marshall discovered gold in California in 1848, it led to the Gold Rush of 1849. (Open Thursday and Sunday, 1 to 4 p.m., from May to October; there is an admission fee.)

35.6   LEFT at the traffic light on South Main Street.
New Hope is rich in history. In 1681, William Penn granted 1000 acres to an Englishman named Thomas Woolrich. In 1700, Robert Heath took possession of the acreage, and, later, 500 acres of the original tract were sold to John Wells, recognized as the actual founder of the town. Wells operated a ferry and tavern, and in 1764 the town was named Coryell's Ferry for John Coryell, who took over as the major landowner in the area. The ferry was important to General George Washington, for it was from this bivouac site that he planned and directed the strategy that led to winning the Battle of Trenton.

Later, after Benjamin Parry built a successful mill operation here, known as "New Hope Mills," the town became known as New Hope. Standing on Main Street in the center of town at 35.7 miles is the Parry Mansion where Benjamin Parry lived until his death in 1839. Ten rooms, each furnished from a different period spanning from the late eighteenth century to the early twentieth century, may be seen. Five generations of Parrys lived here over a period of more than 200 years.

(Call (215) 862-5880 for hours; there is an admission fee.)

The Lenni-Lenape Indians would probably be shocked if they saw how much New Hope has changed since they walked its trails. On weekends, you'll have to weave around swarms of people and dodge auto traffic since it is jammed with shoppers who hunt for clothing, food, jewelry, furniture, crafts, antiques, paintings, toys, and sculpture. (Shops are open from 10 a.m. to 5 p.m. and some evenings during summer and Christmas season.)

A short distance to the left stands the Bucks County Playhouse, the former Parry gristmill, which now serves as the State Theatre of Pennsylvania. Plays, musicals, ballet, and concerts are presented here year round.

36.0   RIGHT onto New Street.

You may want to stop and take a ride into the past via a mule-drawn barge. As you cross under old wooden bridges and travel through the locks of the canal, which opened in 1832, you'll get a glimpse of the oaks that once sheltered George Washington's soldiers. Perhaps you will gain a feeling for what it was like when huge boats plied this water transporting coal and other products. (Open from April to October; there is an admission fee.)

36.3   LEFT at the "T" on Mechanic Street.

36.4   RIGHT at the stop sign on Stockton Street.

Cross Ingham Creek; jog left, and then right.

At Sergeantsville you'll cycle through New Jersey's only covered bridge.

36.5   RIGHT on Bridge Street.
Cross the Delaware back into Lambertville.

37.0   RIGHT at the "T."

37.1   LEFT at the sign for Hopewell via Route 518, then an immediate LEFT on (unmarked) Quarry Street.
A long climb, lasting about 1.8 miles, is followed by a pleasant downhill section, then some hills. You are now on Rocktown-Lambertville Road. Use caution as you cross busy Route 31, then continue straight ahead on Rocktown Road. Lush woods provide relief from the hot sun during summer.

43.0   Right on Mountain Road.
Be careful of loose rocks along this shady road.

44.0   LEFT at the stop sign on Linvale Road.
Daylilies line the side of the road during summer months on this downhill stretch.

45.0   RIGHT at the "T" on Rocktown Road.

45.2   RIGHT at the sign for Neshanic on Route 602.

47.4   LEFT on Route 609.
After a climb of about 0.4 mile, the reward is an excellent vista of surrounding farm country and horse farms.

48.2   RIGHT on Welisewitz Road.
Beautiful rural vistas extend to the left.

49.1   LEFT on Cider Mill Road.
Back Brook runs beneath the narrow bridge. It's a good spot to stop and cool off your feet or rinse your face. Watch out for sharp curves at about 0.9 mile along this road.

50.9   LEFT at the "T" on Clover Hill Road.

51.8   RIGHT at the "T" on 514 Spur.

52.0   STRAIGHT on Route 613 as the 514 Spur turns off to the left.
Cross the bridge over the South Branch into the sleepy town of Three Bridges. This is Main Street; you can purchase a drink at the Three Bridges General Store.

53.6   Bear LEFT in accordance with the bold arrow, then cross Route 202 almost immediately.

53.8   RIGHT on Lazy Brook Road.

55.5   LEFT at the "T" on unmarked Locust Road.

55.7   RIGHT at the "T" on Barley Sheaf Road.

56.6   RIGHT at the "T" on Route 629, Pleasant Run Road.

57.7   LEFT on Hillcrest Road.

60.2   LEFT at the "T," and then another LEFT at the "T" on Route 620.
You'll pass the Readington General Store where you can purchase provisions.

63.6   LEFT at the "T" on Route 523.

63.7   RIGHT on Dreahook Road.
Woods, fields, and a few houses line this road.

67.2   LEFT at the stop sign on Stanton Mountain Road.
A panoramic view is off to the right. If you need supplies, there's a general store as you turn the corner.

67.5   RIGHT on Route 629.

69.0   LEFT on Cratetown Road.

69.6   LEFT on Route 31, then RIGHT on Hibbler Road.
Use caution on Route 31; it's a main thoroughfare.

70.3   LEFT at the "T" on (unmarked) Lilac Drive.
After travelling through a wooded area, railroad tracks appear on the right in a short distance.

71.5   RIGHT at the "T" on (unmarked) Stanton Road.
Cross the railroad tracks, then the South Branch.

72.2   LEFT at the "T" on Old Clinton Road.
As you admire the views on the left, don't forget to watch out for woodchucks that may be crossing the road.

73.5   LEFT on River Road.
A steep downhill stretch leads to a sharp curve.

74.4   LEFT on (unmarked) Route 31.
USE CAUTION: Even though the road isn't marked, it's recognizable by the traffic whizzing by in both directions.

74.8   RIGHT on West Woodschurch Road.
You can rest from this steep hill very shortly; you'll arrive at the entrance to Deer Path Park at 75.3 miles.

Bicycle shops:
Pete's Bike Shop, Route 31, Flemington, (908) 782-5935.

11

Westfield and the Watchungs

Location: Union and Somerset counties
Starting point: Echo Lake Park
Terrain: Moderately difficult with some steep hills
Traffic: Light to moderate
Round-trip distance pedaled: 28.6 miles
Highlights: Miller-Cory House, nature museum.

A blend of parks, neighborhoods, and open spaces, this route passes through several towns in western Union County before climbing into the scenic Watchung Mountains.

Union County earned a reputation for its sparkling air during the nineteenth century, attracting vacationers who eventually established roots here. Railroads, towns, and houses quickly sprouted. Although communities seem to hug one another and the air is no longer so pure, wise officials took pains to set aside a good deal of land for parks, golf courses, and wildlife preserves.

Following bicycle paths through county parks takes you through a variety of affluent neighborhoods. The ride is particularly pleasant on weekends, but traffic is heavy during weekday rush hours, so plan accordingly.

Terrain is largely flat during the first section of the ride. The few hills aren't difficult, but once you cross Route 22, you'll come to the Watchung Mountains. Although these are low enough to qualify as hills rather than mountains, they are a challenge to cyclists.

The trip begins at Echo Lake County Park on Mill Lane, just west of Springfield Avenue. This 139-acre park has two lakes and offers boating, fishing, picnicking, and ice skating. Choose a place to park near the Springfield Avenue side and pedal to Springfield Avenue. The mileage count begins at the junction of Mill Lane and Springfield Avenue.

0.0   RIGHT on Springfield Avenue.

After crossing the small bridge near the park entrance, walk your bike across the road. Continue straight ahead along the gravel path; a stream is to your immediate left and a large nursery is on the right.

0.1   Continue STRAIGHT ahead on the paved bicycle path.

This paved trail is also used by joggers and hikers. At 0.2 mile, you'll come to a pretty pond on your left and will see stands of cattails on the right.

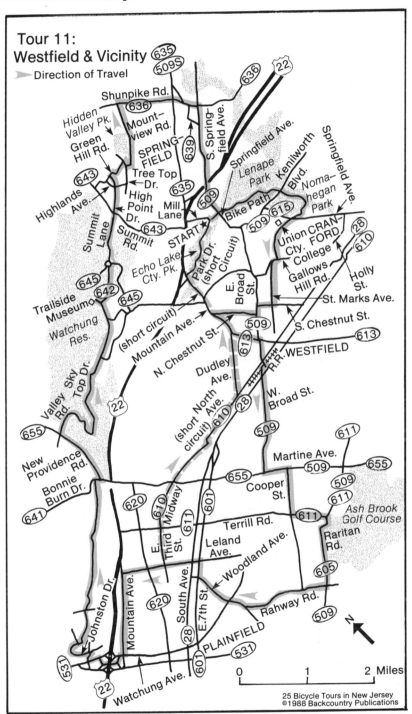

Tour 11:
Westfield & Vicinity
▷ Direction of Travel

Shunpike Rd.
635
509S
636
636
Hidden Valley Pk.
Mount-view Rd.
Green Hill Rd.
SPRING-FIELD
639
S. Springfield Ave.
Springfield Ave.
Kenilworth Blvd.
Springfield Ave.
643
Tree Top Dr.
635
Lenape Park
Noma-negan Park
Highlands Ave.
High Point Dr.
Mill Lane
509
Bike Path
615
509
Union Cty. College
CRAN-FORD
28
Summit Lane
643
Summit Rd.
START
Park Dr. (short Circuit)
Gallows Hill Rd.
610
Holly St.
645
642
645
Echo Lake Cty. Pk.
E. Broad St.
St. Marks Ave.
Trailside Museum
Watchung Res.
(short circuit)
Mountain Ave.
N. Chestnut St.
Dudley Ave.
509
613
613
S. Chestnut St.
Valley Rd.
Sky Top Dr.
22
655
(short North Ave.
circuit) 610
28
W. Broad St.
R.R. WESTFIELD
509
New Providence Rd.
Bonnie Burn Dr.
641
620
610
E. Third St.
Midway
611
601
655
Cooper St.
Martine Ave.
509
611
509
655
611
Ash Brook Golf Course
Terrill Rd.
611
Leland Ave.
Woodland Ave.
Raritan Rd.
620
South Ave.
E.7th St
605
Johnston Dr.
Mountain Ave.
28
Rahway Rd.
509
531
601
PLAINFIELD
531
N
22
Watchung Ave.

0   1   2 Miles

25 Bicycle Tours in New Jersey
©1988 Backcountry Publications

1.0   CROSS Kenilworth Boulevard. and turn LEFT, taking the bicycle path.
The path circles through Nomahegan Park. Cycling along, you'll pass
several places with bike route signs pointing in one direction; bear
right whenever a choice is presented. You'll come to the first right turn
after about 0.1 mile; the path will take you along a quiet tree-lined
street into Cranford.

Architecture buffs might want to detour here to look over some of
the Gothic Revival houses, such as the charming house found at 110
Holly Street. Sometimes called the "pointed style," the lines carry the
eye upward to a steep gabled roof edged with carpenter's lace
bargeboards and clustered chimneys. You may want to stretch at one
of the fitness stations along this route.

1.8   RIGHT across a wooden bridge over the Rahway River, then take the
next TWO RIGHT TURNS.
The trail follows a small, scenic pond. During the summer, lily pads,
pickerel weed, and weeping willows growing alongside are a welcome sight, along with the sounds of chirping birds overhead. This is
a good rest spot for a snack, and rest rooms are available.

2.3   LEFT off the bike route; CROSS Springfield Avenue into the entrance to
Union County College.
Cranford's Union College was the first junior college in the United
States to be established with federal funds. Follow the college road as
it weaves through the campus, past students and Canada geese on
the vast lawns, keeping an eye peeled for its continuation on the other
side of Parking Area 2. Here it passes the William Miller Sperry
Observatory, open certain days to observe the heavens. For hours,
call (201) 276-3319.

3.4   RIGHT at the "T" on Gallows Hill Road.
Pass a cemetery on the right and the attractive Holy Trinity Greek
Orthodox Church on the left. In 1782, convicted murderer James
Morgan was hung on Gallows Hill Road. Considerate of nearby
spectators, his last words to the hangman were, "Do your duty and
don't keep these folks shivering in the cold."

3.6   LEFT on St. Marks Avenue.
This is one of the lovely streets of Westfield, with well-kept houses and
large, old trees. Paul Robeson played baseball and basketball at
Westfield High for a couple of years around 1910, while Mary Pickford
was busy making silent movies here.

4.2   RIGHT on South Chestnut Street.

4.4   LEFT at the "T" on East Broad Street, then an immediate RIGHT on
North Chestnut Street.

5.1 **LEFT at the "T" on Mountain Avenue.**

On the left, after 0.2 mile, is the Miller-Cory House dating to the 1700s. This farmhouse, now a museum staffed by volunteers in period dress, is open only on Sunday afternoons from September to early June. Cooking, crafts, and other day-to-day activities of the early residents are demonstrated. There is an admission fee, call (201) 232-1776 for more information.

Farther down the avenue, just before the junction with East Broad Street, is the historic Presbyterian Church.

6.0 **RIGHT on East Broad Street.**

Along Broad, you'll pass the castle-like Methodist Church on your right, followed by a World War I memorial, before entering an underpass beneath the railroad. BEAR RIGHT immediately afterward.

6.5 **LEFT on West Broad Street.**

7.9 **LEFT on Martine Avenue.**

This is a busy, wide road.

8.3 **RIGHT on Cooper Street.**

There are lots of trees and stately houses along this quiet street in Scotch Plains, named for the Scots who first settled here in the late 1600s.

8.9 **LEFT at the traffic light on Terrill Road.**

9.4 **RIGHT on Raritan Road.**

USE CAUTION—this road is narrow and curving. Follow your nose and you'll pass the entrance to the zoo on the right. On the left is the huge Ash Brook Golf Course, a mecca for golfers and bird-watchers.

The William Miller Sperry Observatory on the grounds of Cranford's Union College is open to the public certain days to observe the heavens.

10.4   RIGHT on Rahway Road.

> This road is narrow and full of potholes. It has many large, old trees and large houses. After 0.5 mile you will pass a castle-like house and begin to climb a long steep grade.

11.7   RIGHT on Woodland Avenue.

12.5   RIGHT on East 7th Street.

12.7   LEFT on Leland Avenue.

> Pass Burger King at junction with South Avenue.
>
> **Alternate Route:** To short circuit this trip and return to the starting point, TURN RIGHT on East 3rd Street, continue straight on Midway Avenue, TURN LEFT at the "T" on North Avenue, LEFT on Dudley Avenue, LEFT on Mountain Avenue; take Park Drive (on the right) into Echo Lake Park. To continue the entire trip, follow the directions below:

13.9   LEFT at the "T" on Mountain Avenue.

> Look for the "elf" house with a large clock on its right side at the junction with Norwood Avenue.

15.1   RIGHT on Watchung Avenue.

15.2   LEFT on ramp onto bridge crossing Route 22 and then LEFT at bridge exit, following signs to Watchung.

15.6   RIGHT on Johnston Drive.

> There's a grocery store on the left at the intersection. This road is very steep, narrow, curving and in generally poor condition; this is the most difficult section of road on the trip and a real challenge. After about a mile of climbing, pull to the right side for your reward: a rest, a drink, and a view of the towns you have pedaled through. Here all of eastern New Jersey stretches before you on the plain below. Church steeples and houses seem to poke through gaps in the trees. The houses atop Johnston Drive have nicely forested lots, and a few are perched on the hillside with commanding views. Continue along Johnston Drive. The road begins to head gently downhill at first, but then it becomes much steeper.

18.8   RIGHT on Bonnie Burn Road, then a quick LEFT onto New Providence Road. Use extreme CAUTION as traffic is fast; many accidents have taken place at these intersections.

> A mining operation comes into view here as the road climbs steadily and steeply.

19.9   RIGHT on Valley Road.

> The name changes to Sky Top Drive. It's a steep climb for the first mile as the road winds through the Watchung Reservation. The setting is

magnificent, and in summer the large trees offer wonderful shade, although it's somewhat dark here even in the middle of a sunny day. During the fall you'll see a rainbow of color along this road as the leaves change color.

22.7   **LEFT at entrance to parking lot for the Trailside Museum.**
Inside the museum, you can fill up your canteen, use the rest room, and view the changing exhibits, including a mineral collection, shells, and other artifacts. (Open September to June, daily 1 to 5 p.m.; July and August, Monday through Friday, 10 a.m. to 5 p.m.; Saturday and Sunday, 1 to 5 p.m.; no admission charge.) When you are ready, return to the road and turn LEFT, continuing in the same direction as before; the road name changes to Summit Lane.

23.3   **RIGHT at the circle; take the second road (toward Summit).**

24.1   **STRAIGHT across Summit Road, onto High Point Drive.**
You're now cycling through a prosperous section of Springfield Township. During the Battle of Springfield in 1780, when local soldiers ran out of gun wadding, Reverend James Caldwell cleverly gave them a bunch of hymn books, not to use for singing but to make gun wadding from their pages!

24.4   **Jog LEFT on Highlands Avenue, then immediate RIGHT to continue on High Point Drive.**

24.6   **RIGHT on Green Hill Road.**

24.9   **RIGHT on Tree Top Drive, then immediate LEFT on Mountview Road.**
Pedal uphill, then enjoy a steep downhill ride. USE CAUTION as this road leads abruptly to the Shunpike intersection.

25.9   **RIGHT at the "T" on Shunpike.**

26.8   **RIGHT on South Springfield Avenue.**
Stay on this road as it continues weaving on. It passes several stores and gas stations. Cross Route 22 at 27.3 miles using extreme CAUTION!

28.6   **RIGHT on Mill Lane into Echo Lake Park.**

Bicycle shops:
J.F.'s Bike Shop, 233 Somerset, North Plainfield, (908) 753-6643.
George's Bicycle Shop, 123 Watchung Avenue, Plainfield, (908) 757-0300.
T.C. Cycles, 728 Clinton Avenue, South Plainfield, (908) 756-1449.
The Bike Stand, 360 Park Avenue, Scotch Plains (908) 322-9022.
Jay's Cycle Center, 227 North Avenue, Westfield, (908) 232-3250.
Pro Tour Cycles, 405 South Avenue, Westfield, (908) 232-0430.

12

Raritan River

Location: Somerset County
Starting point: Raritan Valley Community College
Terrain: Somewhat hilly
Traffic: Light
Round-trip distance pedaled: 36.1 miles
Highlights: Scenic river, farmland vistas, historic houses and roads, flea market.

The Raritan River was recognized by writers and poets as long ago as the 1600s for both its beauty and commercial importance. The Indians discovered it long before and named it Laletan, meaning forked river. They used it as their chief route of travel by canoe until the mid-eighteenth century, when Dutch settlers arrived and harnessed sections of the river to power the wheels of gristmills.

The trip traverses both the North and South Branch of the Raritan, passing near the area where they both join to form the Raritan River. There is also an opportunity to see two historic homes and a flea market.

The tour begins at the lovely campus of Raritan Valley Community College, formerly Somerset County College, located north of Route 22 in Branchburg. Take Campus Drive from Route 614 and park in lot 5. From here you'll be high on a hill facing a picturesque countryside. Set your odometer to zero at the stop sign as you exit from the parking lot.

0.0   **RIGHT on the access road, then LEFT at two "Y"s onto Campus Drive.**
Go downhill, following the main road back to the campus entrance. At 0.6 mile, there will be a building on the left and a small duck pond on the right.

0.9   **LEFT at the "T" on Route 614 east.**
Crossing the North Branch of the Raritan River along this level road, you'll enter Bridgewater Township at 1.9 miles. Indians travelled this river until the mid-eighteenth century; today the North Branch, which begins in Morris County, is once again used by canoeists.

2.1   **RIGHT on Milltown Road.**
Cross Route 22 with caution; it's an extremely dangerous divided highway with fast moving traffic. You'll pass a cornfield on the left; while this stretch of the road has little traffic, it's narrow with no shoulder. The road veers sharply to the right at 3.1 miles at the sign

for North Branch Park. If you're here at the right time, firemen will be practicing pole climbing, jumping, and other maneuvers at the nearby Firemen's Training Center. It's fun to watch. Cross Route 202 at 4.0 miles.

5.2   RIGHT at the "T" on Old York Road.
After pedaling uphill for awhile, you'll cross the North Branch of the Raritan River for the second time at 6.0 miles. This is a very pretty spot where you can look out upon a scenic expanse of farms. It's a good place to open your canteen or dunk your feet.

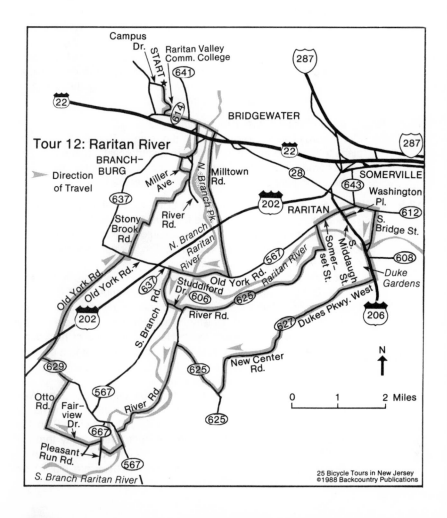

25 Bicycle Tours in New Jersey
©1988 Backcountry Publications

6.5   LEFT on South Branch Road (Route 567).

Farm buildings and barns with silos lie ahead. The River Lea Farm makes a bucolic vista.

7.3   LEFT on Studdiford Drive (Route 606).

Here you'll cross the South Branch of the Raritan River, a favorite stream of trout fisherman and popular with canoeists.

7.6   LEFT at the "T" on River Road.

Follow the lovely South Branch north as it heads downstream to converge with the North Branch at a place the Indians called Tucca-Ramma-Hacking, "the meeting place of the waters." This nicely shaded area is a cool place to rest during summer months. After a short stretch beside the river, the road goes through open country, affording a feeling of spaciousness. Although this scenic stretch of road has no shoulder, there is barely any traffic. You will encounter some hills before coming next to the river again; where the North and South Branch meet, the river is officially known as the Raritan. Find a tree to sit under and enjoy the view before crossing the one-lane bridge over the Raritan at 11.5 miles.

11.7   RIGHT on Somerset Street (Route 626).

Many stores line this busy street in the town of Raritan. It's a good place to buy food and drink. St. Paul's Evangelical Lutheran Church, at the corner of Doughty Street, has beautiful stained-glass windows. At the traffic light at 12.3 miles, cross Highway 206.

12.5   RIGHT on South Middaugh Street and LEFT on Washington Place.

Take an hour off for a free guided tour through the historic Old Dutch Parsonage and the Wallace House located on this street. You can lock your bicycle in the parking area. The curator has generously offered cyclists use of rest room facilities.

The Parsonage was built in 1751 for John Frelinghuysen, Minister of the Dutch Reformed Churches in the Raritan Valley. Here, Frelinghuysen established a theological seminary where young men could be trained for the ministry. When Frelinghuysen died three years later, his wife married Jacob Hardenberg, one of his young students. After becoming a minister, Hardenberg became a staunch supporter of the patriotic cause, frequently entertaining General George Washington at the Parsonage.

At the Wallace House, built in 1775, you'll learn about John Wallace, a Philadelphia tea merchant, and how he rented his home for four months to General Washington for $1000 in 1778. (Both the Wallace House and the Parsonage are open Wednesday through Friday 9 a.m. to noon and 1 to 5 p.m., Saturday 10 a.m. to noon and 1 to 5 p.m., and Sunday 1 to 5 p.m. Both houses are closed on holidays.) Afterward retrace the way you came along Washington Place.

12.8 **RIGHT on South Middaugh Street, then RIGHT on Somerset Street.**
The road joins Somerville's main thoroughfare (Route 28). At 13.3 miles stands the attractive old stone United Reformed Church.

13.5 **RIGHT on South Bridge Street.**

14.2 **LEFT on Route 206.**
USE CAUTION: there is usually lots of traffic. Stay to the right on the highway. The entrance to Duke Gardens is on the right.

Tobacco tycoon James Buchanan Duke bought 400 acres of land here in 1893 along the banks of the Raritan and by the turn of the century had increased his holdings to 2200 acres. His daughter, Doris, inherited his millions and turned the estate into magnificent enclosed greenhouse gardens open to the public. (Closed summer months; a fee is charged.)

The bridge at Neshanic Station leads to the Neshanic flea market, held weekends.

14.9 RIGHT on Dukes Parkway West.

Pedaling on this scenic road, which eventually becomes Route 627, is a pleasure. Continue along this road; at 17.8 miles it turns sharply to the right and becomes New Center Road. It passes through a rural area with lots of farms and fields.

19.6 RIGHT at the "T" on Route 625.

This traffic-free section is bumpy, with no shoulder.

21.0 LEFT at the "T" on River Road.

Cross the South Branch at 21.9 miles on this level, scenic stretch. At 23.0 miles, cross the South Branch again.

23.5 LEFT at the "T" on Route 567.

The South Branch is to your right.

23.7 RIGHT across an iron one-lane bridge.

You've entered quaint Neshanic Station. Just after crossing the bridge look on the left; this is where the Neshanic flea market is held on the weekends. It's a good place to purchase fresh fruit, old tools, books, and a bunch of other assorted goodies. A nearby snack bar provides refreshments and a rest room; you can fill your canteen here.

24.1 RIGHT on Pleasant Run Road (Route 667).

24.3 LEFT on Fairview Drive.

You'll encounter a steep hill at the beginning of this stretch. Follow the road as it bends sharply to the right, continuing straight ahead as its name changes to Otto Road. This shoulderless section is very narrow; it offers nice views of fields, cows, and houses along the left.

26.6 LEFT at the "T" on Route 629.

27.4 RIGHT on Old York Road.

As you turn right, the historic marker designates that you're in Centerville on historic Old Post Road, half-way between Philadelphia, Pennsylvania, and Elizabethtown, New Jersey. Back in the 1700s, the Swift-Sure Stage Coach Line stopped here overnight.

A steep hill lies ahead. At 27.9 miles, cross Route 202 continuing straight ahead, up and down hills, still on Old York Road.

30.3 RIGHT at the "T," continuing on Old York Road.

30.4 LEFT on Stony Brook Road.

Cycling through suburban neighborhoods with no traffic and gentle bends in the road is enjoyable on this stretch.

32.7 LEFT at the "T" on River Road.

This is one of many roads with this name; it's the third one on this trip.

32.8   LEFT on Miller Avenue.

33.4   RIGHT at the "T" on Route 637.

At 34.1 miles, cross under Highway 22.

34.4   LEFT at the "T" on Route 614.

35.2   RIGHT entering grounds of Raritan Valley Community College.

The climb is steady as you follow the campus road. You'll reach the starting point at 36.1 miles.

Bicycle shops:
Gregg's Bike Town, 134-B East Main, Somerville (908) 725-2060.
International Bicycles, 254 US Highway 206, South Somerville (908) 359-2700.

13

Princeton

Location: Somerset and Mercer counties
Starting point: Colonial Park
Terrain: Mostly flat; some hills
Traffic: Light
Round-trip distance pedaled: 51.6 miles
Highlights: Princeton University campus, Colonial Park, Delaware and Raritan
Canal, historic towns.

Many of the quaint, quiet towns you'll be visiting on this trip have changed very little since Washington and his troops passed through in 1777. It's a good idea to get an early start since there are so many historic sites and interesting locales along the way. In addition, scenic roads will take you alongside three serene bodies of water — Lake Carnegie, the Delaware and Raritan Canal, and the Millstone River.

Park at Colonial Park near the village of East Millstone, in the parking lot next to the arboretum and Van der Goot Rose Garden, which is reached via Mettler's Road from Amwell Road (Route 514).

Before starting, you may wish to limber up by strolling through the award-winning one-acre rose garden that features more than 4,000 rose bushes, including hybrid teas, gradiforas, floribundas, climbers, miniatures, old-fashioned, and botanical roses. (Open from 10 a.m. to dusk until Labor Day; then to 4:30 p.m.; there is no admission charge.) A fast walk through the arboretum is also a treat; specimens include dwarf conifers, lilacs, and Japanese flowering cherries.

Reset your odometer at the entrance to the rose garden.

0.0   STRAIGHT, returning to Mettler's Road.

0.1   LEFT on Mettler's Road, then an immediate RIGHT onto the bike path.
This path leads to many activities within the park, including tennis, golf, and a special Par Course Fitness Circuit. Pretty ponds, surrounded by pine trees and weeping willows, are usually teeming with ducks and geese.

1.4   LEFT at the "T" on Elizabeth Avenue.

2.8   LEFT on School House Road.
This narrow road is nearly traffic-free on weekends, but be careful of

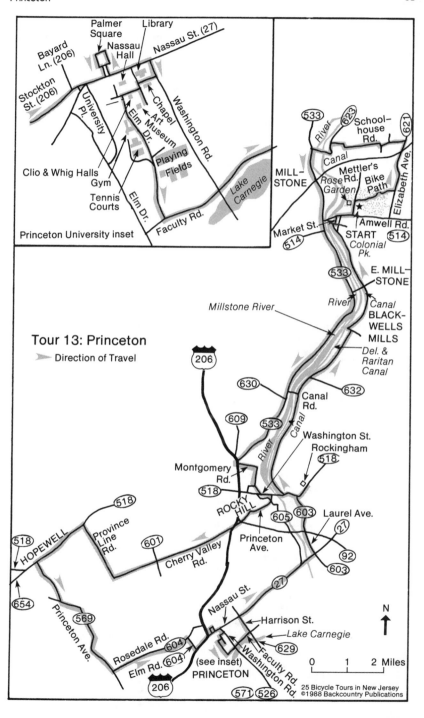

Princeton University inset

Tour 13: Princeton

Direction of Travel

25 Bicycle Tours in New Jersey
©1988 Backcountry Publications

0 1 2 Miles

N

loose gravel in some places. You'll pass pleasant industrial buildings and corporate headquarters.

4.9 **LEFT at the "T" on (unmarked) Route 623.**

Stay with this road as it crosses the Delaware and Raritan Canal and then the Millstone River.

5.7 **LEFT at the "T" on Route 533.**

For food or drink, stop in at Krauszer's at 7.8 miles. This pleasant country lane is very scenic after its junction with Route 514. The northerly flowing Millstone River almost touches the road. During fall, the foliage resembles an artist's palette.

15.6 **LEFT at the "T" on Route 206, then an immediate LEFT on Montgomery Road.**

Stay on Montgomery Road as it swings into quiet Rocky Hill, settled in 1701.

17.1 **LEFT on Washington Street.**

Here you'll pass the First Reformed Church, built in 1857, and places to buy a snack or lunch.

17.3 **RIGHT at the First Aid Squad on (unmarked) Princeton Avenue.**

Fields and many large homes line this road. When you come to Route 206 again (at 18.5 miles), there's a gas station with drinks and rest room facilities available. After crossing this intersection, the road name changes to Cherry Valley Road. During summer months, a canopy of leaves overhead provides relief from the heat.

22.4 **RIGHT on Province Line Road.**

Pedaling here is equivalent to being on a roller coaster.

24.1 **LEFT on Route 518.**

This road takes you into Hopewell, which has stayed much the same as it was when founded in 1706. The gingerbread houses are an architectural buff's delight.

25.5 **LEFT on Princeton Avenue, Route 569.**

Should you wish to take a break, there's a park on the right in about one-quarter mile. Farther down the road is an AT & T facility and the location of the creator of the dreaded college entrance examinations, the Educational Testing Service.

29.9 **LEFT on Rosedale Road (Route 604) into Princeton.**

Settled by Quakers on land William Penn purchased in 1693, Princeton's lush tree-lined streets beckoned dozens of wealthy people, including Grover Cleveland, at the turn of the century.

32.3 **RIGHT on Elm Road staying with Route 604.**

32.8 **LEFT on Route 206 (north).**

As you get into the downtown area, look to your left for the Battle Monument, a local landmark. Nearby stands Morven, a Georgian-style mansion, circa 1750, that served for many years as the home of New Jersey governors.

33.4 **STRAIGHT on Route 27.**

33.5 **LEFT on Palmer Square East.**

Many people, thinking it would hurt local businesses, opposed Princeton businessman Edgar Palmer's desire to knock down a 12-square-block area in 1935 to erect Palmer Square, a group of fancy shops. Not only did his venture prove highly successful, but the square has recently undergone an expansion. Browsing in these elegant shops is always a delight.

When you're finished cycling around the square, turn right toward the one-way traffic sign, and keep making left turns until you come to Palmer Square West. Follow this street out, back to Nassau Street.

33.8 **LEFT on Nassau Street (Route 27).**

You'll find numerous shops where you can browse or purchase food and drink. On your right is Princeton University.

34.0 **RIGHT on Washington Road.**

Turn right onto the first walkway in less than 0.1 mile. The John Foster Dulles Library of Diplomatic History on the right stands opposite an

The Princeton University Art Museum has an impressive 16-foot-high Picasso sculpture, *Head of a Woman,* outside.

unusual sculpture. Carry your bicycle up the ramp in front of you, on the left side of the staircase, for a look at the impressive "Song of the Vowels" sculpture.

Bike racks, available at this location, can be used if you want to walk over to the Gothic-style University Chapel and nearby buildings. The chapel, dedicated in 1928, can seat more than 2,000 people on pews made from army surplus wood originally designated for Civil War gun carriages. The oak paneling, carved in England from Sherwood Forest trees, was from the same wood Robin Hood may have used. On sunny days you'll be able to appreciate the grandeur of the stained-glass windows within the chapel.

To continue by bike, turn left, crossing in front of the chapel. Choose the path that takes you to the left of the Theater in Time. Further ahead, slightly to the right, is the University Art Museum and its marvelous outside 16-foot-high Picasso sculpture, "Head of A Woman," demonstrating the qualities of Cubism for which Picasso is famous. Housing collections of old master prints and drawings, Chinese and early Italian paintings, and pre-Columbian art, this museum is definitely worth a stop.

When finished, take the path leading straight away from the museum entrance, and stay on it as it turns left to Nassau Hall. This large, stone building, considered one of the largest buildings in the colonies, played an important role in our nation's history. Not only did Nassau Hall survive attack during the Battle of Princeton in 1777, but it served as the nation's temporary capital during the time the Continental Congress convened here in 1783. Used for nearly half a century to hold Princeton's classrooms, dormitories, library, chapel, dining room, and kitchen, it now houses the university's offices.

Opposite stand twin Greek temples, Whig and Clio halls, designed in marble and erected in 1893 for the American Whig and Cliosophic Society, the nation's oldest college literary and debating clubs. Both societies have since merged, and the halls are now used for student debates and speakers.

Continue ahead, turning left at the corner on Elm Drive, cycling past several buildings, including the gymnasium, tennis courts, and playing fields.

35.0   LEFT on Faculty Road.

This road takes you past Lake Carnegie, a good place to rest, have a snack, or watch boating activities. The three-and-one-half-mile-long lake, formed by damning the Stony Brook and the Millstone River at Kingston, was a gift to the university from industrialist Andrew Carnegie in 1906. Carnegie, upset by the injuries suffered by football players, hoped rowing would become the new sport. The lake's 2,000-yard course is considered one of the finest in the East.

35.9 LEFT on Harrison Street.

36.5 RIGHT on Nassau Street.

Lake Carnegie shortly comes into view again. As you enter the quaint town of Kingston, you see the Millstone River on one side and the Delaware and Raritan Canal on the other. The canal, scooped out by Irish immigrants using picks and shovels, was built to transport Pennsylvania coal. At its height in 1866, mules along the towpath pulled more than 100 barges a day along the canal; by 1932, the canal was abandoned because of the railroad. Now a state park, it is used for bicycling, hiking, and canoeing.

38.8 LEFT on Laurel Avenue, Route 603, at the traffic light.

Prepare for a long uphill climb.

40.4 RIGHT on Route 518.

40.9 LEFT at the entrance to Rockingham.

General Washington stayed here as a guest of the Berrien's while he drafted his "Farewell Orders to the Army." (The mansion is open Wednesday, Friday, and Saturday; there is no admission charge.)

41.1 RIGHT on Route 518.

After about half a mile you'll begin a refreshing, long downhill stretch.

42.0 RIGHT on Canal Road.

The Delaware and Raritan Canal is on your left along this entire stretch. The maples turn brilliant colors during autumn in this area. You'll soon pass Griggstown—don't worry about exceeding the weight limit on the one-lane bridge at 47.0 miles unless you've had a huge lunch. You'll come to a "T" at 47.3 miles; jog left, then right, and continue on Canal Road.

Blackwells Mills, at 48.6 miles, and several other towns along the canal were active during the days when the canal was a main route for commerce. You'll come to the end of Canal Road in the tiny community of East Millstone where the road suddenly curves to the right, leaving you on Elm Street.

50.5 LEFT on Market Street.

50.7 RIGHT at the "T" on Amwell Road.

51.1 LEFT on Mettler's Road.

51.5 LEFT at the entrance to the arboretum parking lot in Colonial Park.

The entrance to the rose garden is just ahead at 51.6 miles.

Bicycle shops:
Jay's Cycles, 249 Nassau Street, Princeton, (609) 924-7233.
Kopp's Cycle, 38 Spring Street, Princeton, (609) 924-1052.

14

Around Assunpink

Location: Mercer and Monmouth counties
Starting point: Mercer County Park
Terrain: Mostly flat
Traffic: Light
Round-trip distance pedaled: 40.0 miles
Highlights: Horse and sheep farms, fishing, Victorian architecture, bird-watching.

Hurry to take this trip while the area still retains so much of its rural charm. Many communities have been recently built and dozens of houses are under construction, but this easy trip traverses sections of Mercer and Monmouth counties with still undeveloped farmland and wooded areas. Mercer County Park, the county's showplace, offers an excellent, scenic bicycle trail to limber up on at the beginning of the trip.

Within the Assunpink Fish and Wildlife Management Area are five man-made lakes stocked with catfish, largemouth bass, sunfish, and pickerel. Although hunting and fishing is emphasized, Assunpink is considered one of the best birding areas in central New Jersey. If you bring binoculars along, you may spot a turkey vulture, hawk, warbler, or sparrow. During the fall, hunters can usually be seen stalking the abundant deer, rabbits, squirrels, and grouse that roam freely through the Refuge.

Park at the East Picnic Area in Mercer County Park off Route 526, just west of its junction with Route 535 in the hamlet of Edinburg.

0.0   **STRAIGHT on the paved bike trail through Mercer County Park.**
         The trail begins at the edge of the parking area and meanders through this 2,500-acre park, which includes picnic areas, playgrounds, tennis courts, playing fields, and a lovely lake used for canoeing, sailing, and rowing. You'll pass huge oak trees, a blanket of wildflowers during spring and summer months, and you will no doubt spot squirrels and chipmunks as they dart out along the path. Head straight ahead when in doubt about which way to go.

3.3   RIGHT at the end of the bicycle path on Hughes Drive.

4.0   RIGHT at the "T" on Quakerbridge Road.

4.7   RIGHT on Village Road West (which becomes Village Road East).
         This smooth road goes past open fields and houses. Stay with it as it turns sharply. Cross Route 535 at 9.1 miles.

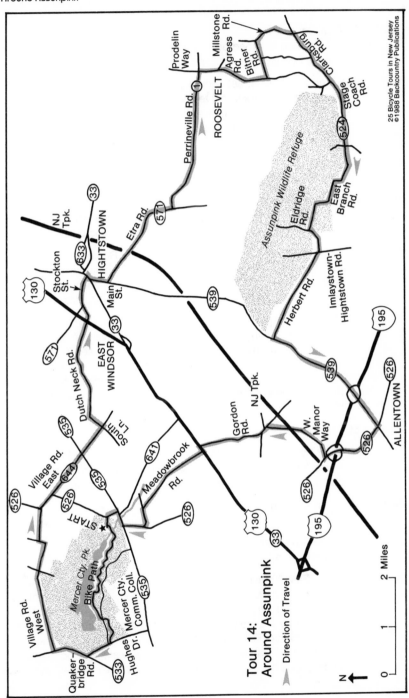

Tour 14:
Around Assunpink

➤ Direction of Travel

N ◀━

0   1   2 Miles

9.8   **LEFT on South Lane.**

Continue on this road as it turns into Dutch Neck Road, which then passes through an East Windsor housing development.

12.7 **RIGHT on Stockton Street (Route 571) in Hightstown.**

Many wealthy people moved to Hightstown during the mid-1850s because of its location midway between Perth Amboy and Burlington. Stockton Street has prime examples of the fine Victorian houses built here during that period.

13.2 **RIGHT at the "T" on Main Street. Stay left, taking Route 571.**

Peddie School and several mansions are on the left.

13.7 **LEFT, still following Route 571 (Etra Road).**

The road is narrow here but in good shape. After passing Etra Lake on the left, stay with Route 571 as it makes some sharp turns.

17.0 **LEFT on Perrineville Road (Monmouth County Route 1).**

It's slow going while pedaling uphill, but the farms provide nice scenery to take your mind off aching muscles. Continue on this road as it makes a sharp right just before Prodelin Way comes in on the left.

19.2 **Bear RIGHT on Agress Road.**

You're now skirting the municipality of Roosevelt. In the 1930s, a factory and dozens of flat-roofed cinder block houses were built as a social experiment in cooperative living for needle-trade workers. The village never succeeded as a self-sufficient community, but today Roosevelt looks much the same as it did originally, and it is home to many writers and artists.

20.3 **LEFT on Bitner Road.**

21.2 **RIGHT at the "T" on Millstone Road.**

Horse farms abound; if you pull over to the fenced pastures for a closer view, one of the horses will usually come over.

22.1 **RIGHT on Clarksburg Road.**

The road climbs steeply at first, and is narrow with a sand shoulder.

23.3 **Bear RIGHT on Stage Coach Road.**

You're now in the midst of sheep farms.

25.3 **RIGHT on East Branch Road.**

This road takes you through a stretch of pretty country as it crosses a corner of the Assunpink Wildlife Refuge, a 5,400-acre reservation managed by the New Jersey Department of Environmental Protection's Division of Fish, Game, and Wildlife. At the center of the refuge are man-made lakes that support a warm-water fish population, including largemouth bass and chain pickerel. Unfortunately you'll have to walk to the lake because the park road is too rocky to cycle over.

East Branch Road twists sharply in places. At 26.8 miles, it turns sharply to the left as Eldridge Road comes in from the right. Go straight through the intersection with Imlaystown-Hightstown Road at 27.4 miles (no road signs). This will take you onto Herbert Road.

29.5 **LEFT at the "T" on Route 539 (south).**

There is a deli at 31.8 miles. Continue ahead to the center of Allentown.

32.5 **RIGHT on Route 526 (west).**

Cross Route 195 and look for the first genuine road (not an entrance or exit for the freeway) on the right. This is West Manor Way. If you come to the New Jersey Turnpike, you've gone too far.

33.8 **RIGHT on (unmarked) West Manor Way.**

35.3 **LEFT at the "T" on Gordon Road.**

This smooth, deserted road is very pleasant to cycle.

36.9 **LEFT at the "T" on Route 130 (a divided road with heavy traffic); then an immediate RIGHT on Meadowbrook Road.**

39.0 **RIGHT at the "T" on Route 526.**

39.4 **RIGHT at the "T," then left in about 0.2 mile, still following Route 526.**

39.8 **LEFT at the entrance to the East Picnic Area of Mercer County Park.**

The parking area is just ahead at 40.0 miles.

Bicycle shops:

Speedway Bicycle Shop, State Highway 33, Hightstown, (609) 443-3320.

You will see horses grazing throughout your trip around Assunpink.

15

Rutgers

Location: Middlesex and Somerset counties
Starting point: Johnson Park
Terrain: Mostly flat
Traffic: Moderate
Round-trip distance pedaled: 42.2 miles
Highlights: Rutgers University campus, gardens, historic houses, Delaware and Raritan Canal, art museum, East Jersey Old Towne.

This trip explores sections of Rutgers University and, to add some spice, some of the nearby towns and open country farther south.

Many of the roads are heavily travelled, especially during rush hours. Although the area is less crowded on the weekend, East Jersey Olde Towne is open only during the week. The display gardens are most interesting during spring, summer, and early fall.

Park at the Olde Towne parking area off River Road (Route 18) in Piscataway along Johnson Drive, opposite Hoes Lane. If you like, spend about an hour exploring Olde Towne. It is open Monday through Friday, 10 a.m. to 3 p.m.; there is an admission charge. Call (201) 463-9077 for further information.

The village, set up to show how English and Dutch farmers lived in the area during the Revolutionary War period, is made up of 20 buildings that stood in different parts of central New Jersey. Among them is the FitzRandolph House, circa 1743, an example of a house built by a farmer new to the area; the Dunn Farmhouse, circa 1745, typical of a successful farmer's house; and the Runyon House, a 1780 mansion containing 17 rooms.

The idea for the restored nineteenth-century village first took shape when Dr. Joseph Kier learned that the Indian Queen Tavern, a historic New Brunswick meeting place built in 1686, was going to be to be torn down. Dr. Kier purchased it for one dollar. Later, Middlesex County set aside several acres of land in Johnson Park to house the village, while money from private sources was used to purchase additional buildings.

Afterwards, walk your bike to the large map of the fitness track, located to your right as you face Olde Towne's buildings. Reset the odometer and prepare to take the bike path just in front of you (right next to the parking lot) toward the left, with the buildings on the right as you pedal.

0.0   LEFT (west) on bike trail; then bear RIGHT.

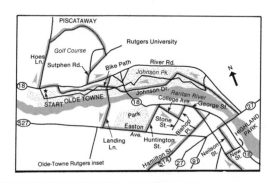

Olde-Towne Rutgers inset

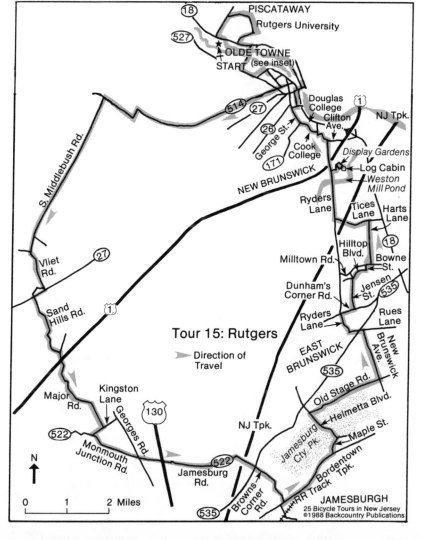

Tour 15: Rutgers

Direction of Travel

0   1   2 Miles

25 Bicycle Tours in New Jersey
©1988 Backcountry Publications

The bike trail ends shortly. Cross River Road onto Hoes Lane from the park path. This narrow road is busy at times and its surface has many large patches and holes.

0.6   RIGHT turn at first road just after the golf course entrance.

This road circles around with a lush green golf course to the right and Rutgers' Busch Campus to the left. You'll pass the Waksman Institute of Microbiology, named in honor of the scientist who pioneered the discovery of several antibiotics, as well as the Rutgers Medical School, the College of Pharmacy, the physics building, and the Hill Computer and Math Center.

1.8   RIGHT on Sutphen Road.

A football stadium is on your left, while a huge bubble dome and several fields used for athletics are on the right.

2.2   LEFT on River Road. Use extreme caution at this busy intersection.

2.6   RIGHT on Landing Lane, the first road leading right.

As you approach the bridge, look for a dirt path on the right and take it across. The span goes over the Raritan River and the Delaware and Raritan Canal. (Watch out for poison ivy, which grows thickly here.) Continue straight ahead at the traffic light at the end of the bridge.

3.2   LEFT at the traffic light on Easton Avenue (Route 527).

This is a dangerous intersection; USE CAUTION.

3.7   LEFT on Huntington Street just past the park.

4.1   RIGHT on College Avenue.

You are now on the College Avenue Campus of Rutgers University. The first large brick building on the left is Alexander Library. Farther along on the right are the gymnasium and student center, which has a restaurant and pizza parlor in its basement. Standing opposite the student center on your left is Brower Commons, which has a snack bar.

4.4   LEFT on Bishop Place (opposite Stone Street on the right).

4.6   RIGHT on unmarked George Street, at the end of Bishop Place.

Johnson and Johnson's corporate headquarters are on the left.

4.9   RIGHT on Hamilton Street.

Stop for a visit at the Zimmerli Art Museum just past the corner on your right. Lock up at the bike rack a short distance down the street. As you walk back toward the museum, notice the lightoliers in front of the Department of Art History building. They were a gift of the class of 1888. Check your helmet and other belongings at the desk and wander leisurely through the tastefully designed exhibit halls.

When finished, cross the street and walk to your right to visit Old

Queens, the large brick building with a cupola. This is where the university began in 1766. Members of the administration, including the president, now use it as an office building. Next door stands the Geology Museum; though worth a visit, its hours are erratic.

Continue cycling southwest along Hamilton Street as it changes from city to suburbia. There is a deli at 9.5 miles.

9.7 **LEFT on South Middlebush Road at the Middlebush Reformed Church.**
This road passes beautiful fields and stately houses. Use caution over the long, narrow bridge. Eventually the road narrows, changes to Vliet Road (no shoulder) and curves to the left.

14.8 **RIGHT at the "T" on Route 27.**

15.0 **LEFT at Sand Hills Road.**
You'll see housing developments at first, but after joining Major Road and crossing Route 1, trees and fields come into view.

18.7 **RIGHT at the "T" on Kingston Lane.**

19.1 **LEFT at the "T" on Monmouth Junction Road.**
This road changes names several times, but don't be concerned because there are very few signs anyway. Stick with it. Snacks are available at 19.3 miles on Georges Road. Cross over the New Jersey Turnpike, heading toward quiet Jamesburg.

24.3 **LEFT on Bordentown Turnpike.**
With a name like Bordentown Turnpike, you might expect a multi-lane road with traffic lights and possibly a traffic cop. Surprisingly, this is just a small street that is easy to miss if you're not careful. Look for Musso's Restaurant on the right where you have to turn. We hope the restaurant sign will still be there when you decide to take this trip. If you reach railroad tracks in the town of Jamesburg, you've gone about a half mile too far.

25.9 **LEFT on Maple Street.**
Pass Helme's Snuff and Tobacco Factory, housed in a tall, austere, brick building.

26.4 **LEFT on Helmetta Boulevard (no sign).**
Pedal through Jamesburg County Park, which has a lovely grouping of plants and trees.

27.2 **RIGHT on Old Stage Road.**
This narrow road is almost void of houses at first, but developments take over as you continue.

29.0 **LEFT on New Brunswick Avenue.**
You are now in East Brunswick, a highly developed suburban area.

30.2   LEFT at the "T" on Rues Lane.

30.5   Bear RIGHT on Ryders Lane.

31.0   RIGHT on Dunham's Corner Road.

31.3   LEFT on Jensen Street.

32.1   RIGHT on Hilltop Boulevard.

32.5   LEFT at the "T" on Bowne Street, then RIGHT at the "T" on Milltown Road.

32.8   LEFT on Harts Lane.
This is an industrial area.

33.8   LEFT on Tices Lane.

34.6   RIGHT on Ryders Lane.
At 35.3 miles cross Weston Mill Pond. Be careful on the bridge.

35.6   RIGHT on side road to Rutgers Display Gardens and Log Cabin.
Road signs point the way past magnificent holly trees, planted in 1927. This is a good place to stop for a while and browse at the flower and azalea gardens. During spring, the azaleas are spectacular in bright shades of purple, pink, red, and blue. Continue to the end of the road to the parking lot at the log cabin perched on a hill overlooking Weston Mill Pond. If you have time, take a short walk in Helyar Preserve. Then turn around, retracing your path back to Ryders Lane.

36.8   RIGHT on Ryders Lane.
Cross Route 1 and continue until the road ends.

37.5   LEFT on Clifton Avenue.
Follow this road through part of the campus of Cook and Douglass colleges. At Cook College, students specialize in agriculture and environmental science. Douglass is currently a college for women only, although the classes are coeducational with other Rutgers University students.

37.9   RIGHT on George Street; then make first U-turn.
Clifton Avenue dumps you onto George Street, where you must turn right. After entering this road, make the first right turn at the U-TURN sign. Then go left at the traffic light, so you will be heading back toward the heart of New Brunswick on George Street.

38.9   RIGHT on New Street, then LEFT on Neilson Street.
If you have time and are hungry, stop at one of the small restaurants on George Street.

39.3   RIGHT on Albany Street (Route 27).

Use extreme CAUTION as traffic can be heavy here. Watch out for cars that wish to turn to the right directly in front of you. Your goal is the bridge across the Raritan River, which is straight ahead. It is probably best to cross the bridge using the pedestrian walkway.

39.6 **LEFT on bicycle path, immediately after crossing Albany Street Bridge.** You are now in the university town of Highland Park. The bike path runs to the left of River Road as you head back toward the starting point. At first the path is alongside the road, but then it wiggles, finally bringing you into Johnson Park, a long, narrow recreational center on the Raritan's north bank. Continue on the path within the park, eventually crossing Landing Lane.

42.2 **ARRIVE at Olde Towne parking lot.**

Bicycle shops:
Highland Park Cyclery, 137 Raritan Avenue, Highland Park, (908) 572-6775.
Kim's Bike Shop, 137 Albany Street, New Brunswick (908) 846-3880.
Stan's Bicycle Shop, 89 Main Street, South River, (908) 257-1890.
Franklin Bicycle Center, 853 Hamilton Street, Somerset, (908) 249-4544.

Benjamin Franklin and John Adams often stopped in at the Indian Queen Tavern, circa 1686. The tavern, purchased by Dr. Kler for $1.00, was the beginning of the East Jersey Olde Towne re-created village that visitors can now tour.

16

Monmouth Battlefield

Location: Monmouth County
Starting point: Monmouth Battlefield State Park
Terrain: Slightly hilly
Traffic: Light to moderate
Round-trip distance pedaled: 41.2 miles
Highlights: Monmouth Battlefield State Park, Turkey Swamp State Park, nature trails, paddle boating, fishing, canoeing, flea market, historic sites.

Ready, aim, duck . . . especially if you begin this trip on June 28. That's when troops gather at Monmouth Battlefield State Park to reenact what was considered to be the longest sustained combat of the Revolutionary War. Although neither the British nor Continental Army could clearly claim victory at the end of the battle, both sides deserved a standing ovation for their courage during eye-to-eye combat.

Events leading to this battle began during the spring of 1778, when the British began evacuating Philadelphia after learning that France had sent troops to help the Continental Army. However, the British didn't plan well; not only did they burden themselves by carrying enormous amounts of supplies on a 12-mile-long wagon train, using valuable manpower to safeguard these possessions, but they also suffered under the weight of their heavy packs and uniforms.

Washington (who luckily wasn't sleeping anywhere at the time) quickly assessed the situation. Realizing that his soldiers were well trained, with new uniforms and equipment, he ordered them to put up road blocks, destroy bridges, and do anything to further weaken the enemy.

You'll be pedaling past ground where Alexander Hamilton, Aaron Burr, Molly Pitcher, and other famous people fought. Born in New Jersey of German descent in 1754, Molly's real name was Molly Ludwig Hays. When her husband, John Hays, was assigned duty in New Jersey, she stayed with him through the battle, helping him and his company by carrying water during the extreme June heat.

Soldiers referred to her as "Molly with the pitcher" and the name stuck. When her husband suffered from heat exhaustion and could no longer fire his cannon, she replaced him, later receiving a commendation from Washington and an army pension—long before the women's liberation movement.

Park your car near the Visitor Center in the large lot at Monmouth Battlefield State Park, off Route 33. Spend some time inside the Visitor Center, where several automatic color slide presentations and an electronic scale model map of the area depict troop movements during the battle. There is no admission charge; the center is open daily except major holidays. The center overlooks the fields where a great part of the conflict was waged. Limber up before your ride by strolling down Combs Hill and try to imagine what took

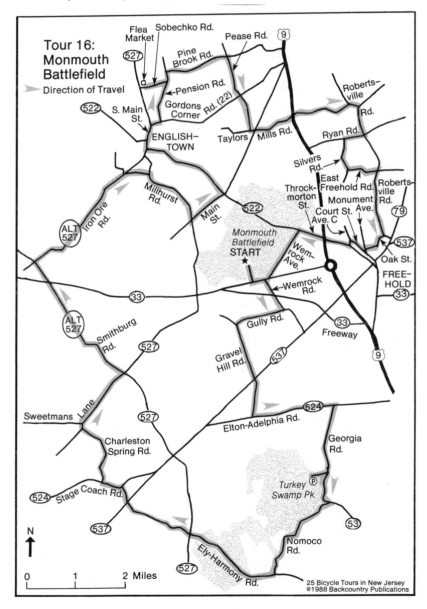

25 Bicycle Tours in New Jersey
©1988 Backcountry Publications

place here. A bridge crosses the marsh, leading on to the battlefield. If you care to walk farther, try the short nature trail, which is excellent during springtime when skunk cabbage, purple violets, maples, and the songs from resident warblers and frogs create just the right mood before cycling.

Reset your odometer to 0.0 at the stop sign at the exit from the main parking lot.

0.0   STRAIGHT ahead on the park road toward the entrance on Route 33.

0.5   LEFT onto Route 33.
          This road is wide but extremely busy.

0.7   RIGHT at the first traffic light onto Wemrock Road.
          Wemrock Road is a fairly wide road with moderate traffic. USE EX-
          TREME CAUTION as you cross the Route 33 Freeway; an entrance
          ramp to the highway crosses the right lane, and motorists sometimes
          enter the ramp at high speed.

1.4   RIGHT on Gully Road.
          This lightly travelled, narrow side road has more than its share of ruts
          and holes, but the wooded areas and apple orchards make up for it.

2.4   Sharp LEFT on Gravel Hill Road.
          Some uphill pedaling is required on the first stretch of this lane. After
          about half a mile, the road levels out, taking you through open
          farmland.

4.3   LEFT at the "T" on Elton-Adelphia Road.
          This is a wide road with moderate traffic changing from farmland to a
          suburban area.

6.0   RIGHT on Georgia Road at sign for Turkey Swamp Park.

7.7   RIGHT at the entrance to Turkey Swamp Park.

8.0   LEFT into the main parking lot, near the park office.
          Lock your bike here; rest rooms are available at the side of the
          building. The park, located on the northern fringe of the Pine Barrens,
          takes its name from the town of Turkey, now known as Adelphia. The
          area is unique, according to the Monmouth County Park System
          brochure, "for although the soil is very sandy, the water table lies just
          beneath the surface, giving rise to swampy conditions whenever the
          surface topography dips to the water line; [hence] the 'swamp' in the
          name Turkey Swamp."
          If you wish, you can take a two-mile bike ride through the park on a
          gravel maintenance road to get a feel for the area. The land within the
          park is nearly flat; the geologic formations are composed of sands
          and clays, providing a habitat for scrub oak and young white oaks
          and a thick understory of pepperbush, huckleberries, and blueber-

ries. Tall pitch pines are currently springing up on the fringes of the forest, while sweet gum and aspen also exist in thick stands here.

Should you care to walk through another day, try one of the pleasant, easy trails. We tried the red trail, about one and a quarter miles in length, leading out to the woodsy Wilderness Camping area. There is also a green-blazed, one-mile trail bordering the red trail, also leading to the lakefront area, and a one-half-mile blue trail going to the boat house. You can picnic, fish, canoe, or rent paddle boats. If this bike trip isn't giving you enough exercise, try working out on the new physical fitness trail, which provides a program of cardiovascular conditioning, flexibility routines, and exercises for muscle tone.

After finishing at the park, return to the main parking lot to pick up the mileage and head toward the entrance.

8.3   **RIGHT after leaving park, staying on Nomoco Road.**
This pleasant road winds through pine groves, new houses, and Turkey Swamp Park on the right.

10.4   **RIGHT at the "T" on Ely-Harmony Road.**
This long grade will have you puffing, but gentle hills follow. Traffic is light here; there are broad curves and the road levels, passing through more pines, a few farmhouses, residential houses, open fields, and a fruit stand as you cross Route 537.

14.1   **LEFT at the "T" on (unmarked) Stage Coach Road.**

14.4   **RIGHT on Charleston Spring Road.**
Start by climbing a small hill. The scenery is pleasant, a mixture of thoroughbred farms, horses, and barns. The route follows a winding, slightly hilly road.

15.9   **RIGHT at the "T" on Sweetmans Lane (no sign).**
Follow this uphill for about 0.5 mile on a smooth road past pastureland, although farms are slowly giving way to developments in this area.

17.2   **LEFT on Route 527A (Smithburg Road).**
This smooth, level road goes past a tree nursery, horse farms, and houses as you pedal up small hills. Cross Route 33.

20.1   **RIGHT, following the sign for 527A toward Englishtown.**
Though it lacks a sign, this road is identified as Iron Ore Road on the Monmouth County map. It starts uphill going up and down until it levels out after a long, gentle descent. Open fields may be seen on the left. Stay right on Iron Ore Road at the junction at about 22.5 miles.

23.1   **RIGHT at the "T" on unmarked road, then next LEFT (after 0.1 mile) on Millhurst Road.**
Woods and some houses are on this pleasant road.

24.4   LEFT on Main Street, County Route 3.

25.2   LEFT on Route 522 at the sign for Englishtown.
            This road is a bit busy, but has a narrow, sandy shoulder. Refresh-
            ments can be purchased just before the junction with South Main
            Street in the center of Englishtown.

27.0   RIGHT on South Main Street.

27.4   RIGHT on Gordons Corner Road (Route 22).

27.6   LEFT on Pension Road.

28.4   LEFT on Sobechko Road.
            This road takes you into the famous Englishtown Flea Market. Flea
            markets were named for the fleas that occupied every square inch of
            the areas where merchants sold their wares in open markets. Today
            the fleas may be gone, but be forewarned, the Englishtown Flea
            Market—reputed to be the largest in the state—can be a muddy mess
            after rain or snow. It's best to lock your bike in a dry area and walk
            around to see the huge amount of goodies for sale. It is always fun,
            and it's open year round on Saturday from dawn to 5 p.m., and
            Sunday from 9 a.m. to 5 p.m.
               When you're finished exploring and shopping, return to the corner
            of Sobechko and Pension roads.

28.4   LEFT (north) on Pension Road from Sobechko Road.

28.6   First RIGHT on Pine Brook Road.
            After climbing a small hill, you'll pass woods which may eventually
            become sites for new houses.

29.9   RIGHT on Pease Road at the stop sign.
            Relatively free of traffic, this is a nicely shaded country road.

31.4   LEFT at the "T" on Taylors Mills Road.
            After passing through housing developments, cross Route 9 at the
            stoplight. USE CAUTION: this intersection is usually busy. Here you'll
            begin pedaling along a wide road through an established surburban
            area. The road name eventually changes to Lafayette Road.

33.5   RIGHT at the "T" on (unmarked) Robertsville Road.

34.2   RIGHT on (unmarked) Ryan Road.

34.6   LEFT on Silvers Road.
            Travelling these medium-sized hills provides a good workout.

35.3   LEFT on East Freehold Road.
            On this section you will have smooth pedaling in a lovely neighbor-
            hood.

35.9 RIGHT on Robertsville Road.

After passing horse farms, climb up a long, fairly steep hill heading toward the center of the Borough of Freehold.

37.1 RIGHT on Oak Street.

Follow Oak Street as it curves along.

37.6 LEFT at the "T" on (unmarked) Monument Avenue.

The Monmouth County Court House is to your right. At the corner of Monument Avenue and Court Street stands the impressive Battle of Monmouth statue, designated as a New Jersey State historic site. The panels depict scenes from the Revolution, scenes honoring Molly Pitcher, the Wayne Charge, Washington rallying the troops, and the Council of War at Hopewell. It includes such personages as Lafayette, Washington, and Lord Stirling and has an impressive figure at the top. A time capsule is buried near the monument.

Freehold was settled by Scottish settlers in 1715 who named the area Monmouth and their new village Monmouth Court House. The village quickly gained a reputation as an important agricultural center because the flat land was so fertile. The town was renamed Freehold in 1801.

37.7 RIGHT at the "T" on Court Street.

The impressive Georgian-style stone house on your left is the Monmouth County Historical Association. Stop if you wish to see an excellent collection of American antiques, furniture, textiles, ceramics, firearms, and paintings, as well as the research library chock full of books relating to local history and genealogy. (Open Tuesday through Saturday 10 a.m. to 4 p.m. and Sunday 1 to 4 p.m.; there is an admission charge.)

38.0 LEFT on Avenue C.

38.2 RIGHT on Throckmorton Street (Route 522).

Before going under the Route 9 underpass this road traverses an industrial area.

39.4 LEFT on Wemrock Road.

During apple blossom time these orchards are beautiful; in season you may be able to purchase apples and cider.

40.5 RIGHT on Route 33.

40.7 RIGHT at entrance to Monmouth Battlefield State Park.

Continue straight ahead to reach starting point at 41.2 miles.

Bicycle shops:

Freehold Bicycles, 554 Park Avenue, Freehold, (908) 431-0266.
Fun Town, U.S. Highway 9, Freehold, (908) 780-5750.

17
Sandy Hook

Location: Monmouth County
Starting point: Sandy Hook, Gateway National Recreation Area
Terrain: Flat
Traffic: Light
Round-trip distance pedaled: 11.6 miles
Highlights: Lighthouse, fort, holly forest, swimming.

Sandy Hook offers easy cycling along beautiful dunes, a quiet bay, and pounding ocean surf. Another bonus in cycling "The Hook" is the opportunity to relive history. Here you can explore an old fort, enter the site of the first U.S. Lifesaving Station on the Eastern seaboard, and tour one of the oldest continuously operated lighthouses in the country. Topping this off with a walk in the holly forest or going for a swim guarantees a memorable day.

Although it appears to be a peaceful place now, Sandy Hook has had an eventful history. Between 1839 and 1848, roughly 158 vessels were lost off the Jersey shore. The cry for help, "Ship Ashore," was usually futile since there was no plan in effect to save those aboard ship until Congress finally appropriated money to build small lifeboat stations along the Jersey coast.

Farther along your ride, you'll see why Sandy Hook, strategically located at the entrance to New York Harbor, was an ideal place to build Fort Hancock and mortar batteries. While the fort looks much the same as it did when soldiers manned it to protect the harbor, the shape of the sandy spit of land it was built on has changed.

Although the Lenni-Lenape Indians found the same fishing grounds and tasty beach plums that we see today, the contours of "The Hook" keep changing because the ocean carries sand north. The lighthouse originally stood only 500 feet from the water's edge, but it is now about one and a half miles away because of the strong off-shore currents.

The busy season is from Memorial Day to Labor Day, and that's when a fee is charged for parking. Plan on arriving off-season or late in the day when the crowds are gone, and stay to watch the sunset. For information on park programs, call (201) 872-0092.

Park in lot "B," the first lot after entering the park.

0.0   RIGHT (north) on the park road.
     To your left, perched 254 feet above sea level overlooking Sandy Hook Bay, are the impressive Twin Lights of Navesink. Now a histori-

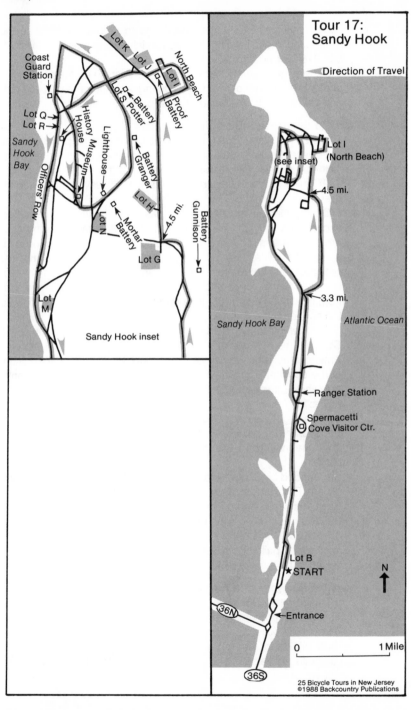

Sandy Hook inset

Tour 17:
Sandy Hook

◀ Direction of Travel

Coast Guard Station

Lot K Lot J Lot I
North Beach
Proof Battery

Lot Q
Lot R
Sandy Hook Bay
History Museum House
Lighthouse
Lot S Potter Battery
Battery Granger
Lot H
4.5 mi.
Battery Gunnison
Officers' Row
Lot N
Mortar Battery
Lot G
Lot M

Lot I (North Beach)
(see inset)
4.5 mi.
3.3 mi.
Sandy Hook Bay
Atlantic Ocean
Ranger Station
Spermacetti Cove Visitor Ctr.
Lot B
★ START
36N
Entrance
N
36S

0   1 Mile

25 Bicycle Tours in New Jersey
©1988 Backcountry Publications

cal and maritime museum, this was once an important lighthouse and radar experimental station. It makes an interesting side trip; call (201) 566-2161 for hours.

On the right, sand dunes and huge boulders keep the ocean from encroaching too far onto the land. During summer months, rest rooms and refreshments are found at most parking lot areas.

1.7   RIGHT to Spermacetti Cove Visitor Center.

This is a "must" stop. Pick up a map and information on programs, and ask to see the ten-minute slide presentation describing the area and historical events. Before leaving, check out the exhibit in this circa 1894 building, which served as the first U.S. Lifesaving Station on the east coast.

During summer months, exciting rescue drills are reenacted here according to government regulations of 1899, complete with period dress and a small bronze cannon once used to fire a rescue line to the flailing ship. The "rescued" people are brought back to land in a breeches buoy: a life preserver with pants attached in which a person sits while being pulled back to safety. This type of rescue was used from the 1800s until 1961. It's a thrill to watch, especially the firing of the cannon.

You'll enjoy taking the Holly Forest Walk just outside the Visitor Center. This 1.5-mile trail is reputed to have the largest stand of American hollies on the eastern seaboard. Prickly pear cactus is one of the dominant plants along the walk, and during summer months they show off spectacular bright yellow flowers. Birds monopolize the hollies during winter when they can be seen diving down into the bushes to get the luscious red berries. There are lots of beach plums, but even more poison ivy, so watch out.

Return to the main road, turn right, and pass through the gate into Fort Hancock.

Surrounded by Sandy Hook Bay, New York Harbor, and the Atlantic Ocean, Fort Hancock was named for Civil War Major General Winfield Scott Hancock. Approximately 18,000 men were garrisoned here in the 1890s, standing watch over gun batteries.

Today the fort looks very much the same as it did in days long gone with every building, street, sidewalk, and bit of lawn planned in advance by the army.

3.3   RIGHT at sign for North Beach.

Park at Battery Gunnison, about 1.1 miles down the road on the right. Explore the gun emplacements and concrete bunkers built in 1904 to protect the coast against possible attack. Six-inch battery guns were built on disappearing carriages; in 1943 they were converted to barbette pedestals. Their steel shields protected the gun crews from machine gun or light cannon fire, while mines, anchored around the entrance to New York Harbor, could be fired electrically from shore.

4.5   **RIGHT at sign for North Beach.**

5.0   **RIGHT onto a deeply-rutted dirt road to Parking Lot I.**
Formed only about 60 years ago by the longshore current, North Beach is a good place to swim, spot shore birds, look for interesting shells, and enjoy the sounds of the ocean.
Follow direction signs out of the lot and continue straight ahead.
On the left is Proof Battery, the army's first proving ground, where, from 1874 to 1919, mortars, field artillery, and machine guns were tested, along with the Lyle gun used for ship rescues.

5.3   **RIGHT at the stop sign, then an immediate left.**

5.6   **LEFT at the stop sign (this is the road just before the street running along the bay).**
Pedal past enlisted men's quarters on the left (on your left as you

Cycle past one of the oldest continuously operated lighthouses in the country at Sandy Hook.

head south). Sandy Hook Museum is on the left, about 0.2 mile down. Through pictures and authentic historical artifacts, this 1899 guardhouse and post jail now serves as a museum, open weekends from 1 to 5 p.m. year round.

5.9   LEFT at the yield sign.

At the next yield sign, the lighthouse looms on the left, while a mortar battery is on your right. This mortar battery, built in 1894, was the first of its kind used for coastal defense. Once inside, you can follow the railroad tracks into one of four identical pits connected by a tunnel. The circles on the floor indicate former sites that once supported large breech-loading mortars.

If the lighthouse is open, sign up for a tour. Built in 1764 to protect ships sailing into New York Harbor, it is the oldest original working lighthouse in the United States. It stands 103 feet tall, and to reach the lantern involves climbing 100 steps plus a 12-foot ladder. While the exterior walls are built of rubblestone, the interior is lined with brick. It is eight feet, six and a half inches thick at the base.

Automated in 1962, the light currently used is a 45,000-candlepower, white electric-fired light that is visible for about 19 miles. In 1964 the lighthouse was declared a National Historic Landmark.

When you are ready to continue, return to the road you were on and turn LEFT after the yield sign in front of the mortar battery.

You'll soon come to Battery Granger and Battery Potter, both on the right side. Although off limits, they're still impressive to look at, having once served as part of New York Harbor's defense system.

This massive bunker complex contained steam-powered hydraulic equipment to raise and lower guns. Neither weapons nor crew were visible from the ocean. The Potter Bunker, disarmed in 1906, is the only fortification of its kind in the United States. The Granger ten-inch rifle could strike a ship eight miles out at sea.

6.5   RIGHT at stop sign, then an immediate LEFT.

The entrance to the Coast Guard station is 0.2 mile ahead. Unfortunately, visitors are not allowed. Stay left, cycling south along the bay. At 6.9 miles you'll see the Rodman Cannon. This impressive weapon is one of two that remain and is reputed to be the largest smooth-bore, muzzle-loading weapon ever cast.

Continue straight along "Officer's Row" overlooking Sandy Hook Bay for a look at houses that differ from the usual army quarters. Normally facing the parade ground, here they were built to face the bay, with officers having the distinction of living in detached houses instead of the normal duplex units.

History House on the left at 7.0 miles is worth a stop. Filled with veterans' memorabilia and photo exhibits, it demonstrates what a model officer's home was like at the turn of the century. (Open weekends from 1 to 5 p.m. year round.)

7.6 **RIGHT at the yield sign; follow the main park road south.**

You'll pass many of the same plants the Indians found here and used as food and medicine: yarrow, for burns and earaches; cattails, for food and padding in pillows; prickly pear cactus, to remove warts; phragmites, enjoyed for its special gum extract; Joe Pye weed, used as a stimulant; and black cherry, used for jellies.

Stop at the small picnic area on the right at 8.1 miles for a short walk along a spit of land protruding into the bay, a favorite hangout for the birds. Your bike can be locked onto the boardwalk fence.

There's a good chance that you'll see lots of birds; "The Hook" is located along the Atlantic Flyway and more than 300 species of birds have been spotted here.

Continue straight ahead back to the starting point.

Bicycle shops:
None on this route.

18

Allaire

Location: Monmouth County
Starting point: Allaire State Park
Terrain: Mostly flat
Traffic: Light to moderate
Round-trip distance pedaled: 26.1 miles
Highlights: Allaire State Park and Village, Manasquan River, fishing, bird-watching.

Though the roar of the blast furnace can no longer be heard, Allaire Village stands as a reminder of the successful bog iron industry in this area over 140 years ago. Allaire Village, where this trip begins, originally housed a sawmill operation in 1750 that was purchased by James Peter Allaire in 1822 for the supply of bog iron to operate his steamboat engine works in New York. Allaire was already a successful man, having built the cylinder for the S.S. *Savannah*, the first steam vessel to cross the Atlantic in 1819.

With Allaire's expertise, the bog iron works flourished; and his village housed approximately 500 workers and their families. Craftspersons included moulders, ware-cleaners, carpenters, pattern makers, wheelwrights, millers, teamsters, one-raisers, stage drivers, grooms, and harness makers. Stoves, screws, pipe, hand irons, pots, and kettles were a few of the articles manufactured here.

Spend awhile taking a self-guided walk through the village for a look at the restored row houses, formerly workers' homes; the mill pond, fed by a stream named Mill Run and built to hold water that served as a source of power for the mill located along the stream bank; and an old wooden farmhouse dating from the 1700s, used by the ironwork's manager. The Episcopal Church Allaire built for the community is unusual. Not only is the steeple situated over the pulpit, but worshippers were not required to pay pew rents. Today it's used for wedding ceremonies.

The bog iron industry declined as hardrock iron ore and anthracite were discovered in Pennsylvania around 1846, and although Allaire's son stayed on for four decades longer, people left the village and it slowly decayed. Thankfully, the state has restored it and today you can see the beehive shaped blast furnace, watch demonstrations at the blacksmith shop, or limber up on one of the short, interesting trails within the park. You may wish to camp inside the park. Call (201) 938-2371 for further information. (The village is open daily; there is a fee for parking from Memorial Day to Labor Day.)

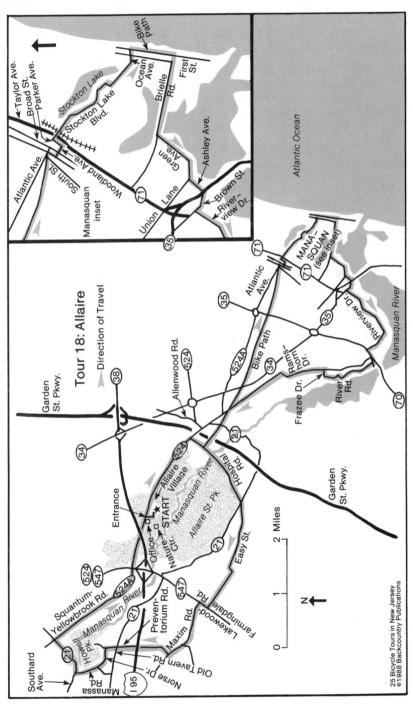

Tour 18: Allaire

→ Direction of Travel

Atlantic Ocean

Manasquan River

Garden St. Pkwy.

2 Miles

N

25 Bicycle Tours in New Jersey
©1988 Backcountry Publications

Manasquan inset:

Taylor Ave.
Broad St.
Parker Ave.
Atlantic Ave.
South St.
Woodland Ave.
Stockton Lake
Stockton Lake Blvd.
Ocean Ave.
Brielle Rd.
First St.
Bike Path
Ashley Ave.
Green Ave.
Union Lane
Brown St.
Riverview Dr.
71
35
Manasquan inset

Main map labels:

MANASQUAN (see inset)
71
35
Atlantic Ave.
Bike Path
Rams-horn Dr.
Frazee Dr.
River Rd.
70
34
Riverview Dr.
Allenwood Rd.
524
524A
38
34
Garden St. Pkwy.
Entrance
Allaire Village
START
Nature Ctr.
Office
Manasquan River
Allaire St. Pk.
Hospital Rd.
21
Easy St.
Squantum-Yellowbrook Rd.
524
547
524A
Manasquan River
Howell H. Pk.
Preven-torium Rd.
Maxim Rd.
Old Tavern Rd.
Norse Dr.
Manassa Rd.
Southard Ave.
21
I-95
Lakewood-Farmingdale Rd.
547
21

Park in the Allaire Village parking lot; pedal to the parking lot exit, and reset your odometer when you reach Route 524.

0.0 RIGHT on Route 524 east.

You might be here in time to see the steam locomotive pass by. Rides are available during summer months.

Just before climbing a gentle hill you'll see the lush green lawn of the Spring Meadow Golf Course, run by the state of New Jersey.

1.4 RIGHT on Hospital Road.

There's a horse farm on this corner; if you have a spare carrot, you won't have to look far to share it.

1.7 LEFT onto the unmarked bicycle path, known as the Edgar Felix Bicycle Path, and identified by a "closed to motorized traffic" sign.

Although power lines along this narrow, slightly rough road are unsightly, the surroundings are pleasant. Almost immediately upon entering, you'll come to a small pond frequented by fishermen. Pine trees, rhododendron, and mountain laurel abound along this former rail line partially obscuring houses set back from the path.

5.1 LEFT at the end of the bike trail in the Borough of Manasquan and an immediate RIGHT on Atlantic Avenue.

You'll find drinks and a rest room at the gas station.

5.4 RIGHT on Broad Street and an immediate LEFT onto (unmarked) Woodland Avenue.

5.5 LEFT on Parker Avenue.

Follow the road as it turns right. Continue straight across Taylor Avenue and the railroad tracks. The street name changes to Stockton Lake Boulevard. If you need food or drink, there is a restaurant on this corner and a soda machine at the liquor store.

Stockton Lake is to your left; it's a good place to sit and have a snack while watching visiting mallards, egrets, and Canada geese. The National Guard Training Center is on the opposite side of the lake.

The road turns sharply right into North Potter.

6.3 First LEFT on Ocean Avenue, continuing straight to the ocean.

6.7 RIGHT on the paved ocean path.

Biking is permitted from October to May, but from June to September bicycles are allowed only between 6 and 9 a.m. During these restricted periods use First Street.

The white sand and blue ocean are a refreshing change of scenery in spite of the tacky amusement section and refreshment stands on the right.

7.1 RIGHT onto Brielle Road (at the rest rooms on the beach).

The marina makes an interesting stop, but be prepared for stiff winds while crossing the drawbridge.

7.7 LEFT immediately after the drawbridge on (unmarked) Green Avenue.

8.3 RIGHT on Union Lane, and the first LEFT on Ashley Avenue.

8.6 RIGHT on Brown Street.

8.7 LEFT on Riverview Drive.

During springtime, this residential neighborhood is ablaze with cherry, crabapple, and dogwood trees. As you pedal along the slightly hilly terrain, you'll pass a golf course, a pond, and many more impressive trees, including magnolias and Japanese maples.

10.3 LEFT on Highway 70; then an immediate right at the fork in the road before the gas station.

10.6 RIGHT on River Road.

The Manasquan River, on the left, was a favorite of the Lenni-Lenape Indians. They named it the "Manatahasquakan," meaning the place where they left their squaws while gathering shellfish at the ocean. They used the tall, straight tulip trees that still grow in these woods today for their canoes. Upstream, the river is known for its tasty trout.

Continue straight through this lovely residential neighborhood. Just before the road ends, look for an unusual house on the left and see if you can figure out what it represents. We're still puzzled.

11.8 RIGHT at the end of River Road on (unmarked) Frazee Drive.

11.9 LEFT on Ramshorn Drive.

14.1 LEFT on the bike path.

If you come to the stop sign at the Allenwood Road junction (opposite the Allenwood Grange building), you've gone too far; turn back and find the bicycle trail under the power lines. Or, if you want a drink or snack, you can visit the Allenwood General Store before returning to the bike path.

14.8 LEFT on Hospital Road.

This is another opportunity to watch the horses as they graze in the pasture if you missed them on the way out. Continue straight as Hospital Road becomes Easy Street.

18.2 RIGHT at the "T" on (unmarked) Lakewood-Farmingdale Road.

18.4 LEFT on Maxim Road.

19.6 RIGHT on Preventorium Road.

Standing at the corner of Preventorium and Old Tavern Roads is the Ardena Public School #2, built in 1855. One of several hills in Monmouth County lies ahead.

20.8 LEFT on Norse Drive (at Police Headquarters).

21.2 RIGHT on Manassa Road.

21.7 RIGHT on Southard Avenue.

22.4 RIGHT on Squankum-Yellowbrook Road.

22.7 RIGHT at the entrance to the Howell Park Golf Course.

Pedal 0.2 mile to the iron bridge erected in 1852. Lock your bike and spend awhile walking the path beneath the bridge alongside the Manasquan River. Spring is the best time of year to find an abundance of wildflowers here. Surprisingly, three different shades of violets can be found—purple, white, and yellow. In addition, there is the beautiful trout lily, a trumpet-shaped yellow flower, and lots of green skunk cabbage poking up in the wet areas. If you smell it, you'll know instantly how it got its name. Although Indians ate skunk cabbage, the plant is poisonous unless boiled several times. One of the first wildflowers of the season, its bloom begins the end of February and magically the snow around it melts as it pops up. Other beauties include the five-petal pink spring beauty, the Jack-in-the-pulpit, trilium, and marsh marigold. You also may be lucky enough to spot a harmless black racer or rat snake or the pine snake that's fond of hanging from tree limbs.

Fall is a good time to study the trees. One worth noting is the ironwood, recognizable any time of year by its smooth, tight bark of wavy and twisting blue and gray bands. Should you swing an axe at this tree, it would probably swing back at you because the bark is so tough.

When finished exploring, return to the park entrance.

23.1 RIGHT on Squankum-Yellowbrook Road.

The entrance to Allaire State Park is at 26.1 miles.

Bicycle shops:

Brielle Cyclery, 205 Union Avenue, Brielle, (908) 528-9121.

Southern New Jersey

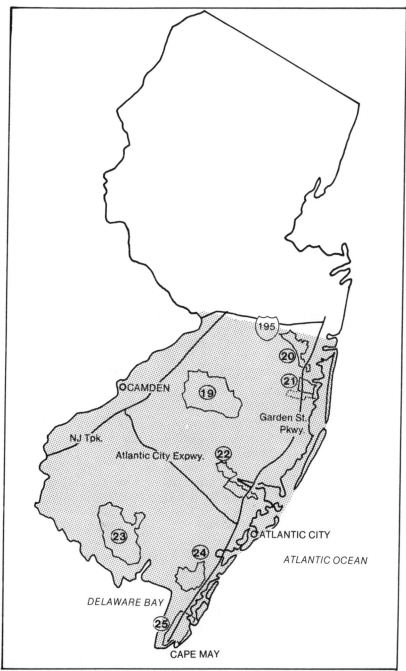

19
Lebanon Forest

Location: Burlington County
Starting point: Mount Holly
Terrain: Flat
Traffic: Light to moderate
Round-trip distance pedaled: 52.9 miles
Highlights: Historic Mount Holly and Smithville, pine barrens, swimming, fishing.

A visit to this quiet section of Burlington County will make you feel as though you've stepped back in time. The trip begins in the historic town of Mount Holly, settled by Quakers from Yorkshire and London in the seventeenth century.

After pedaling past well-preserved buildings in Mount Holly, you continue on to Smithville, former home of the unique "Bicycle Railway," before entering the Pine Barrens and the tranquil Lebanon State Forest.

Park at the shopping center on the east side of High Street just north of the intersection with Levis Drive and Ridgely Street. If you are coming from Interstate 295 or the New Jersey Turnpike (exit 5), take 541 south and make a left onto High Street. The shopping center is on your left. Pedal to the intersection of High Street and Levis Drive, resetting your odometer at this point.

0.0 STRAIGHT (south) on High Street.

High Street, in the oldest section of town, is lined with stately Georgian, Federal, and Carpenter Gothic houses. Stop in at the Mount Holly Visitor Center (at 0.4 mile on your left) if you want a map of local historic sites, such as the Prison Museum at 128 High Street. Built in 1810, this prison and workhouse was the first fireproof building erected in the United States and, until 1965, the oldest prison in continuous use in America. Free tours are conducted Wednesdays and occasionally Saturdays. The interior design, including arched ceiling corridors, thick walls, and iron hardware is very interesting, but also depressing when one considers that prisoners lived in such crowded, cramped conditions.

Next door stands the Burlington County Court House (1796), reputed to be one of the finest examples of colonial architecture in the nation. Farther down the street are the impressive tall spires that identify St. Andrew's Church.

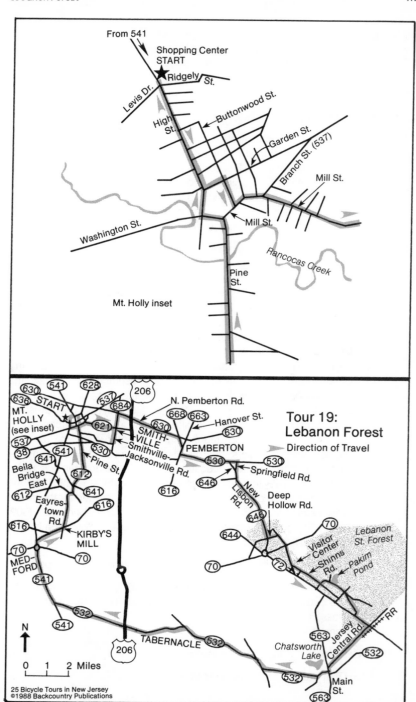

0.7   **LEFT on Garden Street.**
The Friends' Meeting House (1775) on this corner was used for numerous state legislature meetings in 1779. Before that, British troops used it as a commissary; many of the butchers' cleaver marks are still visible on the benches.

0.8   **RIGHT on Buttonwood Street.**

1.0   **LEFT at the "T" on Mill Street.**
Hack's Canoe Rental, established in 1848, (opposite you on Rancocas Creek), was the first canoe rental business in the United States. Inside, three of the original canoes used are displayed.
Bear right at 1.2 miles, sticking with Mill Street as Route 537 veers to the left, after which the name changes to Mount Holly-Smithville Road. Traffic lightens as you enter open country.

3.0   **RIGHT on Smithville-Jacksonville Road.**
The entrance to Smithville is at 3.3 miles. In 1865, Hezekiah Bradley Smith converted an abandoned thread mill here into a thriving machine manufacturing center. While they produced a steam-powered bicycle and a kerosene burning tricycle, one of the company's most lucrative items was the Star bicycle. It differed from all previous high wheelers because it was built with a small guiding wheel in front of the large back wheel to insure greater stability.
After Smith died, his associate built the "Bicycle Railway" to carry workers from Mount Holly to the factory. It resembled a rail fence; the rider simply sat between two wheels working the pedals up and down, instead of in a rotary motion, while a third wheel pressing against the bottom rail kept the bike in balance. At a top speed of 18 miles per hour, the rider reached the factory in minutes. The only problem was that riders had to pull off onto a siding when someone came from the opposite direction because a second rail was never built. The railway enjoyed great fame from 1892 to 1898 until the company declared bankruptcy. (A small fee is charged for tours held Wednesday and Sunday, April through November; call (609) 261-5068 for more information.) After you have explored the bicycle railway, head back to the road.

3.3   **LEFT (north) on Smithville-Jacksonville Road, retracing your path.**

4.2   **RIGHT on North Pemberton Road (Route 630).**
This two-lane highway has a fairly wide shoulder with light traffic. Cross Route 206 at 4.9 miles. Many attractive farms may be seen along this stretch.

7.7   **RIGHT following sign for Pemberton.**

8.1   **RIGHT at stop sign on Hanover Street.**

8.5   LEFT on Route 530.

Leaving Pemberton you encounter a narrow-shouldered section of road. Burlington County College comes up in approximately two miles.

11.4   RIGHT on Springfield Road.

Grazing horses and lovely fields make pleasant vistas.

11.8   LEFT on New Lisbon Road.

The fragrant aroma of pine marks your arrival at Lebanon State Forest, named for the Lebanon Glass Works established here in 1862. This vicinity was perfect for glassmaking because of an abundance of sand and wood for charcoal, but when the supply of wood became exhausted in 1867, the site was abandoned.

As you pedal along this long, quiet stretch of smooth, almost traffic-

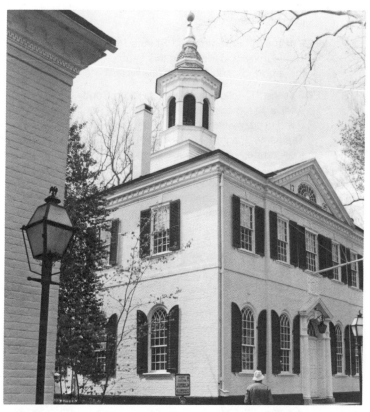

The Burlington County Court House, dating back to 1796, is reputed to be one of the finest examples of colonial architecture in the nation.

free road, it seems as though this part of the county hasn't been touched by time. Sand roads occasionally appear on either side, but unless you explore by foot, where they go will remain a mystery. The Pine Barrens appear awesome to some, but the area isn't really as barren as the name implies; the expression comes from colonial days when land was judged barren if it couldn't sustain traditional crops.

15.8   LEFT on Deep Hollow Road.

Stick with this road as it turns sharply to the right at 16.5 miles; a pond soon appears on the right. This is a good spot to stretch, relax, have a drink, and perhaps soak your feet. After crossing Route 70, you'll come to Lebanon State Forest Visitor Center in about 3/4 mile. Rest rooms are available, along with maps and information. Don't sample the water here unless you're desperate; it has a high iron content and tastes terrible. If you want a bird's-eye view of the surrounding country, inquire about climbing the nearby fire tower before continuing on the same road.

17.9   LEFT at the "T" on unmarked Shinns Road.

The journey is idyllic along this beautiful, peaceful stretch of road as the aroma of pine fills your nostrils.

19.8   LEFT at the "T" following sign for Pakim Pond.

After a little more than a half mile, look for the parking lot at Pakim Pond, a cozy waterhole developed from a former cranberry reservoir. The name "Pakim" is derived from a Lenni-Lenape Indian word meaning "cranberry." Plan on spending awhile taking in the peaceful scene, having lunch, going for a swim, or stretching your legs on the short trail circling the pond.

When finished, continue in the same direction as before, follow the road straight ahead through a campground area, and go around the locked gate when you come to it.

22.6   LEFT on Route 72.

This is a main road; stay on the wide shoulder.

23.6   RIGHT on unmarked Jersey Central Road, just before the railroad overpass.

Void of traffic, but full of potholes, this road follows through pines into Chatsworth.

26.6   LEFT on Main Street, then immediate RIGHT on Route 532.

This is a l-o-n-g stretch, so settle down for pleasant riding through changing scenery along a flat, lightly travelled road sporting a side shoulder most of the way. In about half a mile you'll come to Chatsworth Lake, a scenic body of water surrounded by trees. The ride continues for several miles through pine forest before a second beautiful pond appears on the right side of the road where evergreens seem to grow right up to the water's edge. Farmland and a few private houses provide a change of pace before entering the village of Tabernacle at 36.3 miles. The cemetery here, deeded by William and Sarah Wilkens, is for residents of Tabernacle for as long as the "wheels of time shall not cease to roll."

Go straight after the stop sign at 36.4 miles, continuing on Route 532. Tabernacle is a good place to pick up food and drink; you can also wait until you come to the Country Store at 37.7 miles, just after crossing Route 206. If you need bicycle supplies, stop in at the repair shop at 38.0 miles. For a brief rest at a pretty brook, try Earl Jackson Memorial Park on your left at 41.5 miles.

41.7   RIGHT at the "T" on Route 541.

There are a variety of stores here offering rest rooms and/or food. Stay on Route 541 as the road twists a bit. At Medford use extreme caution at the traffic circle across Route 70. Stay on Route 541 heading north.

45.0   RIGHT at sign for Kirby's Mill.

Continue straight across the intersection at 45.6 miles on Church Road, Route 616 east. Kirby's Mill, a restoration, is a scenic place to stop and cast a line if you have time.

46.7   LEFT on Eayrestown Road.

Huge farms are a delight to see along this stretch.

48.5   RIGHT at the "T" on Bella Bridge East.

48.6   LEFT at the "T" on Eayrestown Road.

Food, drink, and rest rooms are available at the intersection with Route 38. Continue straight ahead, (you're now on Pine Street) back into the center of Mount Holly. Stop just before the end of this street at the firehouse on the right. Next to the modern structure stands the Relief Fire Company No. I, the oldest continuously operated volunteer fire department in the country. In the days before fire engines, an alarm would bring volunteers to the station to get their leather fire buckets. Ask to see some of these ancient implements on display in the museum.

52.0   LEFT at the "T" on Mill Street.

This is a dangerous intersection.

52.1   RIGHT at the traffic light on High Street.

Reach starting point at 52.9 miles.

Bicycle shops:

Genie Cyclery, Skeet & Dixontown Road, Medford, (908) 953-0200.
Chip-N-Dale Bike Shop, 1240 Monmouth Road, Mount Holly, (609) 261-1981.

20
Lakewood

Location: Ocean County
Starting point: Police Headquarters, Oak Avenue
Terrain: Flat
Traffic: Moderate
Round-trip distance pedaled: 36.1 miles
Highlights: Swimming, antiquing, bird-watching, beautiful woods.

There is a humorous side to the merging of the old and the new as communities quickly replace the farms and forests of northern Ocean County. For example, you may see a hand-written sign propped up against the front steps of an old farmhouse offering free horse manure — just across the street from a shiny new housing development.

Although you will rarely experience solitude along these roads, you will, while inhaling the aroma of fragrant pine, capture a little of the remaining beauty that drew the wealthy to Lakewood in the era of the Gay Nineties. Many millionaires, including the Astors, Vanderbilts, Goulds, and Rockefellers, considered Ocean County's pine-scented air to be therapeutic and built their summer mansions around Lake Carasaljo. As the reputation of the area grew, visitors flocked here from miles around. Even today during summer months Lakewood is still a very popular place for boating and swimming.

Begin at the Dover Township Police Headquarters parking lot on Oak Avenue, near the Bey-Lea golf course just north of Toms River. (Large groups should notify the officer in charge.) Reset your odometer at the parking lot exit nearest to the headquarters building.

0.0   LEFT (west) on Oak Avenue.

0.1   LEFT on Bay Avenue.
The Bey-Lea Municipal Golf Course is on your right.

0.4   RIGHT on Bey-Lea Road, Route 571.
As you pedal along the edge of the golf course, enjoy the pleasant vista of green grass and tall border trees.

0.9   RIGHT on Old Freehold Road.

1.5   LEFT on Dugan Lane.

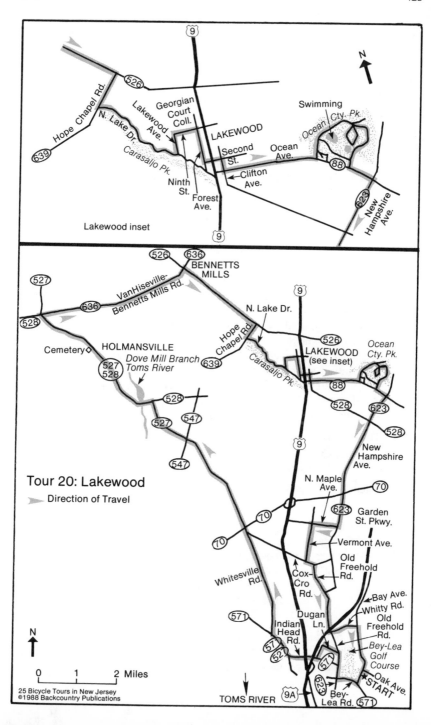

Lakewood inset

Tour 20: Lakewood

Direction of Travel

N

0   1   2 Miles

25 Bicycle Tours in New Jersey
©1988 Backcountry Publications

After passing a residential neighborhood, the road bends and runs parallel to the Garden State Parkway. During summer months you'll probably be pedaling faster than the cars!

2.3   RIGHT at the "T" on Indian Head Road.

Go under the parkway and cross Route 9. Watch out for some interesting obstacles: This wide, busy road is frequented by Canada geese nearly year round. A pond is on your right at 2.8 miles.

3.7   RIGHT on Whitesville Road, Route 527.

Here you'll see examples of new houses and developments as well as remnants of farms and country stores. Woodchucks love to cross this smooth, wide-shouldered road. After crossing Route 70, at 6.4 miles, you'll travel through a wooded area and will pass an antique shop and country store. There is also a small pond along this stretch.

10.4   LEFT at the "T" continuing on Route 527.

The pond at 10.7 miles is a perfect place for a break. This section of the road, which passes by a small dam holding back the Dove Mill Branch of the Toms River, has a broad shoulder. At 12.7 miles, you'll come to the Holmanville Cemetery, founded in 1845.

14.2   RIGHT on unmarked Van Hiseville-Bennetts Mills Road following the sign for Freehold.

After this intersection, just past the Jackson First Aid Station, is the start of a pleasant, uncrowded stretch offering fine country cycling and an exciting, long downhill pass before entering the town of Bennetts Mills. If you didn't take a break at the last pond, there is another opportunity at 17.8 miles.

18.0   RIGHT on Route 526.

Food, drink, and rest room facilities are available here. BE CAREFUL. The road widens to four lanes with lots of traffic and no shoulder.

20.3   RIGHT on Hope Chapel Road.

A chapel and cemetery are on the right at 20.5 miles.

20.8   LEFT on North Lake Drive.

Carasaljo Park, on the right, has magnificent stands of oak, pine, hemlock, and cedar. On your left, there are huge houses sporting beautifully landscaped lawns. In about a mile you'll come to Lake Carasaljo, named by ironmaster Joseph W. Brick for his daughters, Carrie, Sally, and Josephine. Stop at 22.0 miles for a look at the sculpture gardens in Georgian Court College, on the left.

22.3   LEFT on Lakewood Avenue.

These are the grounds of Georgian Court College, a private college. The 200-acre estate, originally owned by New York financier George

J. Gould, is exquisite. Unfortunately, visitors aren't encouraged to tour the grounds, but you can peek in and see quite a bit of the fountains, sunken gardens, and formal gardens.

22.5   **RIGHT on Ninth Street.**

22.8   **RIGHT on Forest Avenue.**

23.3   **LEFT on Second Street.**

23.6   **RIGHT on Clifton Avenue.**
Numerous opportunities to purchase food and drink are available here.

23.7   **LEFT on Main Street (Route 88).**
The road name soon changes to Ocean Avenue. Hold on tight on this section; for about a mile, you'll have to dodge sewer grates, holes, tar patches, and heavy traffic. Fortunately, the next stop makes up for the inconvenience.

24.9   **LEFT into Ocean County Park.**
Cyclists do not have to pay to enter this 323-acre recreational show-

Ocean County Park has delightful cycling trails through wooded areas and a beach and ponds for swimming.

place donated by the heirs of John D. Rockefeller Sr., who once lived on these grounds. The park has more than 150 species of trees and shrubs and a herd of deer. It was also used as the spring training headquarters for the New York Giants baseball team at one time.

Follow the main park road to the swimming area at 25.4 miles. This safe, sandy beach, nestled in the pines, is a delight during summer months.

25.7   RIGHT between wooden posts onto the bicycle path.
This unmarked bicycling path, opposite a long, low building, leads to a beautiful small pond which is an ideal place to sit, relax, have lunch, or identify birds alighting upon tree branches.

25.9   LEFT, following the bicycle path along the pond's edge.
Stay on the path; it turns left less than 0.1 mile after the pond and follows past the Police Academy located on the right.

26.2   RIGHT between wooden posts onto the park road.
As you circle through the park, you'll pass tennis courts, a well-stocked lake, and large playing fields.

27.0   LEFT on Ocean Avenue.

27.4   RIGHT at the traffic light on New Hampshire Avenue.
Traffic is moderate along this smooth road.

30.8   RIGHT on North Maple Avenue.
You may wish to stop and rest at this horse farm for a while. Enjoy the bucolic atmosphere in the midst of a populated area.

31.4   LEFT at the stop sign on Vermont Avenue.

32.3   LEFT on Cox Cro Road.

32.5   RIGHT on Old Freehold Road.
The shoulder is wide on this section. At 33.5 miles, bear right as New Hampshire Road joins in from the left.

34.2   LEFT on Whitty Road.

34.9   RIGHT at the "T" on Bay Avenue.
The Bey-Lea golf course is on the right.

36.0   LEFT on Oak Avenue.
Arrive at the parking lot at 36.1 miles.

Bicycle shops:
Bicycles Unlimited, 67 East County Line Road, Lakewood, (908) 363-2453.
Mone Auto Supply, 244 Main Street, Lakewood, (908) 363-1345.
Padi's Pedal Power, 1177 Fischer Boulevard, Toms River, (908) 270-5920.

21

Berkeley Island and Double Trouble

Location: Ocean County
Starting point: Berkeley Island County Park
Terrain: Flat
Traffic: Light, depending on season
Round-trip distance pedaled: 21.1 miles
Highlights: Swimming, sunbathing, fishing.

This pleasant, leisurely cycling trip meanders through communities bordering Barnegat Bay and the Toms River before reaching Double Trouble State Park. You'll have the opportunity not only to observe boaters, swimmers, and sunbathers, but to join them, depending on your inclination and the season.

Although the Jersey shore is overrun with vacationers during summer months, this route avoids most of the busy areas; spring, fall, or even a mild winter's day are ideal times to cycle this route.

Begin at Berkeley Island County Park, a small, scenic recreation area located on a 23-acre peninsula along Barnegat Bay. The bay offers excellent crabbing and fishing, as well as picnic tables and rest rooms. To reach the park, take Route 9 south of the municipality of Toms River, turn east at the traffic light on Butler Boulevard, and follow the signs. Park your car in the paved parking area, resetting your bicycle odometer when you reach the entrance to the parking lot.

0.0   STRAIGHT ahead (west) on the park entrance road (Brennan Concourse).

0.6   RIGHT on South Bayview Avenue.
At 1.6 miles stay right at the fork. Listen closely; the soft sounds you'll hear in this area are from the huge stands of marsh grasses as they rub against each other in the breeze.

2.4   RIGHT on Bay Boulevard.
This wide road has a good shoulder edged with more grasses and healthy pine trees.

2.5   LEFT on Bayview Avenue.
If you like, use the restaurant on the corner for a pit stop or a quick bite before proceeding. You'll pass through a new neighborhood converted from former marshland. The lawns are worth a look; some

homeowners are using their ingenuity decorating with driftwood, rock, or lush beds of grass. The lagoons are man-made, and most houses at the water's edge are fortunate to have boat slips for easy access to the water. Boat rental places along this stretch usually have soda machines and rest room facilities.

6.7   RIGHT on Ocean Gate Avenue.

The deli and inn on this corner serve food and drinks.

6.8   LEFT on East Chelsea Avenue, which turns into Prospect Avenue.

At about 6.9 miles you'll find a nice spot to rest; a large grassy area is on the left and a small stream faces an inlet to the right.

8.1   RIGHT on Cedar Avenue.

8.4   LEFT on Riverside Drive, at the edge of the Toms River.

The route follows the river for a little more than half a mile. You may wish to stop for a view of sail and powerboats, or to take a swim or walk out onto the pier at 8.9 miles to stretch your legs.

9.0   LEFT on Avon Road.

9.5   RIGHT on Pennsylvania Avenue, which changes to Barnegat Boulevard.

10.4   LEFT at the "T" on Beachwood Boulevard.

10.5   RIGHT on Forepeak Avenue.

10.7   LEFT at the "T" on Starboard Street.

10.8   RIGHT on Atlantic City Boulevard. Make an immediate LEFT, then an immediate RIGHT onto Flint Road.

11.0   LEFT on Dover Road.

11.7   LEFT on Double Trouble Road.

Along this lightly travelled road are lovely stands of pine, oak, and sassafras. Although it parallels the Garden State Parkway, you'll feel far from civilization.

At 15.0 miles, you'll come to the entrance to Double Trouble State Park. The origin of the park's name remains a mystery. Mickey Coen, a naturalist with the Ocean County Parks System, says it was named "Double Trouble" by a preacher and his wife in the 1840s after muskrats dug holes in their dam twice in one week. Architectural historians recently attributed the name to an eighteenth-century saw-mill owner who remarked after being told that spring floods had washed out the dam above his mill for the second time in two days, "Now we have double trouble!"

If you're feeling adventurous and don't mind cycling along sand

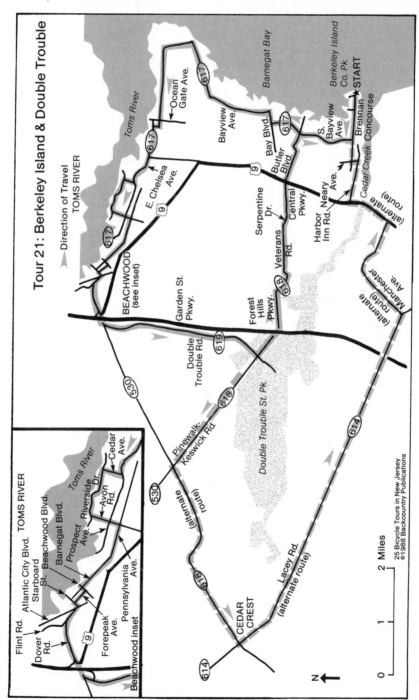

Tour 21: Berkeley Island & Double Trouble

roads, take some time to explore the park. Head over to the circa 1765 sawmill, and if it is in operation, ask permission to stay and watch it work. You'll learn how complicated it is to produce cedar shingles from logs—especially when 1000 shingles are cut an hour using a machine built in 1883! Outside the mill are remnants of a former logging village dating to 1812, when white cedar was logged from surrounding swamps for building ships. After the swamps were cleared, the land was used for cranberry production.

15.0   **LEFT (east) on Pinewald-Keswick Road at the entrance to Double Trouble State Park.**
The route from this point leads directly back to Berkeley Island Park. For a longer trip (by about 16 miles) see the alternate route below.
   Pinewalk-Keswick Road meanders, changing names several times (Forest Hills Parkway, Veterans, Serpentine, Central Parkway), and finally turns into Butler Boulevard where it crosses Route 9 (at 18.5 miles) at a traffic light.

19.4   **RIGHT on South Bayview Avenue (unmarked) at the sign for Berkeley Island Park.**

20.5   **LEFT on Brennan Concourse.**

21.1   **ARRIVE at starting point.**
Alternate Route: If you wish to take the alternate route which adds about 16 miles, make a RIGHT turn at Pinewald-Keswick Road at the entrance to Double Trouble State Park; follow Route 618 to Cedar Crest, and make a LEFT on Lacey Road (Route 614). After crossing the Garden State Parkway, make a LEFT on Manchester Avenue, another LEFT on Route 9, and a RIGHT on Harbor Inn Road. A LEFT on Neary Avenue and a RIGHT on Brennan Concourse will take you back to Berkeley Island Park.

Bicycle shops:
Eckert's Bicycles International, 101 State Highway 166, Beachwood, (908) 349-2333.
Jerry's Bicycle Shop, State Highway 37, Toms River, (908) 929-1155.

22

Batsto

Location: Atlantic and Burlington counties
Starting point: Batsto Village
Terrain: Mostly flat
Traffic: Very light
Round-trip distance pedaled: 44.6 miles
Highlights: Batsto Village, historic Smithville, winery tour, pine barrens, scenic
river.

Our trip starts at Batsto Village where an iron furnace, which operated around the clock two centuries ago, played a key role in the industrial development of the United States by producing iron pots, kettles, and Dutch ovens. Later, when the American Colonies struggled for independence from the British Crown, the furnace was used to make weapons for the Revolutionary Army.

Batsto is derived from the Swedish word "Batstu," referring to a bathing place; it's believed that settlers applied this name to the nearby river that was dammed in 1766 to supply water power to operate four bellows and two hammer wheels in the village. During the War of 1812, the furnace was again used for warfare fittings, but by the mid-1830s, the discovery of coal in Pennsylvania decreased the need for bog iron, and the village began to fail. Plan on spending an hour or two exploring the village before starting out. (Open Memorial Day to Labor Day, 10 a.m. to 5 p.m. daily; Labor Day to Memorial Day, 11 a.m. to 5 p.m. daily; closed Thanksgiving, Christmas, and New Year's Day. There is an admission fee during summer months.)

The rest of the trip is equally as pleasant. Most of the roads, with the exception of Route 643, have little traffic and provide solitude while pedaling. The quiet beauty of the pine barrens is a refreshing change from crowds, and a couple of rewards on this trip are wine sampling at the Renault Winery and a taste of excellent ice cream at historic Smithville Village.

Pedal to the parking lot exit at Batsto Village and reset your odometer.

0.0   LEFT on the (unnamed) park road.

The Batona Trail comes into view at 0.2 mile, and a fire tower is visible at 0.4 mile. The road is so quiet that all you'll hear is the whirr of the bicycle tires and birds chirping in overhead branches. The scent of pine trees is delightful. Although this road changes names several times, you won't notice it because of the lack of signs. It gradually curves around to the right.

5.1   LEFT at the "T" on unmarked Route 542.

This road has some traffic and a wide shoulder. A good place to pick up snacks is at Mike's Country Store at 5.6 miles.

7.4   RIGHT onto unmarked Church Road, just past Korny Korner.

This is the second road going to the right that you come to; there's a road sign indicating "8 feet clearance" as you turn.

8.5   RIGHT at the "T" onto unmarked River Road. Another "low clearance" sign is visible here.

You'll reach the Mullica River at about 8.9 miles, at a private boat launch. Named for Eric Mullica, who settled his Swedish colony on the shores of the river in 1697, the Mullica was the Indians' favorite oyster-gathering place. Today it's a hit with canoeists.

9.2   Follow the road across the wooden bridge.

Fishing from the bridge is a favorite activity. Look for swamp grasses after crossing the bridge and blue flag iris in springtime. Lush groves of pine trees appear again along this straight, smooth road.

11.9   LEFT at the "T" onto Route 563.

Alternate Route: To short circuit this trip, go RIGHT instead and then follow directions at 38.3 miles (see map).

12.0   LEFT on Route 624.

Maples and pines line this long, deserted stretch, until the Port General Store at 18.6 miles.

   Alternate Route: To shorten the trip by 10.8 miles, go right on Leipzig Avenue at 15.9 miles; then make a right onto Moss Mill Road (Alternate Route 561) after 2.3 miles. Follow directions at 31.5 miles (see map).

19.5   RIGHT at the "T" at junction with Route 575. Continue straight ahead on Route 610 East.

19.8   Cross the bridge, then BEAR LEFT following the sign to Smithville.

A side road comes off to the left at 20.6 miles. Bear right at this junction, following the main road.

22.0   RIGHT on Route 9. This will immediately lead to Old Smithville on the right.

The inn, built in 1787, stands in the center of this restored village that includes numerous early American village shops and buildings, a gristmill, and a general store. (Open daily, free.) When through exploring, return to the Route 9 entrance.

22.0   Continue south on Route 9.

22.1   RIGHT turn at first intersection onto Alternate Route 561, Moss Mill Road.

The Pomona golf course provides lush greenery along the way.

31.5   **RIGHT onto Bremen Avenue at the sign for Renault Winery.**

32.2   **RIGHT at entrance to Renault Winery. Proceed to the winery walking your bike along the gravel driveway.**

Lock your bicycle to a post in the parking lot and take some time to explore the winery, reputed to be the oldest continuously operated vineyard in the United States. It was founded in the late nineteenth century by master winemaker Louis Nicholas Renault, a native of Rheims, France. Renault found the soil of south Jersey similar to that of certain vineyards in France and began producing champagne in 1870. While Prohibition spelled the end for wineries, this one prospered thanks to their new product, "Renault Tonic." People rushed to their drugstore to purchase this elixir, advertised as a youth potion and backache remedy, although it was actually a wine in disguise. Cleverly, the company didn't use the word "wine" anywhere on the front label, but on their back label wrote a simple message, "Caution:

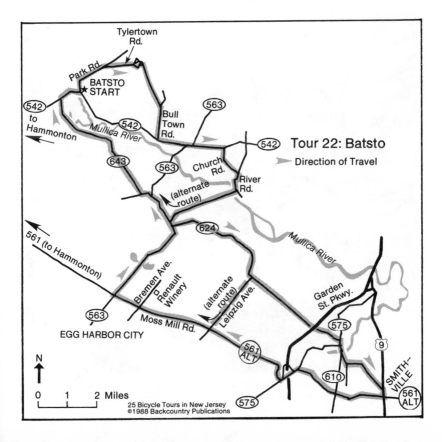

25 Bicycle Tours in New Jersey
©1988 Backcountry Publications

Do not refrigerate this tonic as it will turn into wine."

Today the Milza family owns the winery, and for one dollar you can take a nice break and sample some of the champagnes and wines, including Cold Duck, cabernet sauvignon, and others. You can also tour the Glass Museum, where over 300 champagne glasses are displayed, and look at old wine presses and antique bottling machinery in an Italianate Spanish-style courtyard.

When through, continue to Bremen Avenue, turn left, and return to the junction with Moss Mill Road.

33.1   RIGHT on Moss Mill Road (Alternate Route 561 north).

33.9   RIGHT onto Route 563.

At 35.4 miles you'll see bodies of water on both sides of the road and a campground on the right.

38.3   Continue straight ahead onto Route 643 at the junction of Routes 563 and 643.

Batsto Village offers a look at an old iron furnace, a chance to cast off in the water, and a look at historic buildings.

The scenic Mullica River is adjacent to the right side of the road at 40.9 miles. A store serving drinks is at 41.2 miles.

43.3 **RIGHT onto Route 542.**

44.2 **LEFT at the entrance to Batsto area.**
Arrive at the entrance to the Batsto parking lot at 44.6 miles.

Bicycle shops:
The closest is Pro Pedals, 684 South White Horse Pike, Hammonton, (908) 561-3030.

23

Bridgeton

Location: Cumberland County
Starting point: K-Mart Shopping Center, Vineland
Terrain: Flat
Traffic: Light
Round-trip distance pedaled: 66.0 miles
Highlights: Wheaton Village, Bridgeton Historic District, Parvin State Park.

South Jersey, famous as a glassmaking center since colonial times, continues to thrive today. Wheaton Village, a stop along our route, commemorates the rich history of glassmaking through demonstrations by skilled craftsmen and the exquisite Museum of American Glass.

This section of the state is also known for its truck farming, and you'll see acres of fruits and vegetables along the route which justify New Jersey's nickname, the Garden State. Row after row of tomatoes, potatoes, zucchini, corn, and cabbage stretch out into the distance creating wondrous patterns as you cycle by.

During the first day of this two-day trip, you'll sample bucolic farm scenery, a refreshing swim at Parvin Lake, and an afternoon exploring historic Bridgeton, which lies along the Cohansey River. On the second day, you'll travel south along deserted roads in a semicircle through farmland and marshland to Wheaton Village in Millville.

Park at the K-Mart Shopping Center on the west side of Route 47 (Delsea Drive) in Vineland, near the border with Millville. Cumberland Mall is opposite the highway. Reset your odometer at the exit where it intersects Route 47.

0.0   RIGHT (south) on Route 47.

> Almost immediately, you'll arrive at the intersection with Route 55, a major artery that leads nowhere, according to natives. There is lots of traffic so watch for merging cars in this section.

0.7   Bear RIGHT at the sign for Millville Airport and then RIGHT again on Sharp Street.

> You'll pass a food market at 1.9 miles in Millville before crossing a couple of bridges. Union Lake flanks your right.

2.5   RIGHT on Cooper Street.

2.8   LEFT at the end of the street on School Drive.

2.9   RIGHT at the "T" on (unmarked) Carmel Road.

You'll ride through a forested area on the right for about a half mile before entering farm country. Fortunately, traffic is light here because there isn't any shoulder. If you're here on the right day, you might enjoy festivities held year round at the County Fairground at 6.0 miles.

6.7   LEFT at the "T" on Sherman Road.

6.8   RIGHT on Route 634 at the 4-H sign.

Farms line both sides of this shoulderless road. There is a general store at 9.6 miles and an attractive modern church at 10.5 miles.

11.2   RIGHT on Parvin's Mill Road at the sign for Parvin State Park.

The park entrance is in less than a mile. Rental boats are available at the lake; it's a lovely spot to stop.

12.4   LEFT on Route 540.

This road, the first one after the park entrance, is unmarked, as are many of the intersections in this area. Route 540 follows along the edge of the park, and you'll have views of the lake for a short while. There's a swimming beach at 12.7 miles where you might want to stop for a dip. As you cycle further, you'll pass dense woods, farms, and numerous roadside farm stands.

14.8   LEFT at the "T" as Route 553 joins in.

14.9   RIGHT, continuing on Route 540.

Truck farms abound in this area.

16.6   LEFT on Route 612, Polk Lane.

This smooth, lightly travelled road leads past more farmland. Depending on the season, there will be huge crops of corn, squash, tomatoes, and potatoes.

20.9   RIGHT at the "T" on Route 617.

Serene Seeley Lake is on the right.

21.0   LEFT on (unmarked) Holding Road.

A slight hill comes as a surprise, adding a bit of variety to an otherwise flat landscape. Pickers can often be seen working these farms.

22.1   RIGHT at the "T" on (unmarked) Silver Lake Road.

22.3   LEFT at the "T" on (unmarked) Beebe Run Road.

You'll be passing pleasant scenery along this smooth road.

24.4   LEFT on West Park Drive into the Bridgeton City Park.

24.8   First RIGHT onto (unmarked) Mayor Aitken Drive (Route 697).

The Cohanzick Zoo, on the left at 25.1 miles, is worth a stop. There is

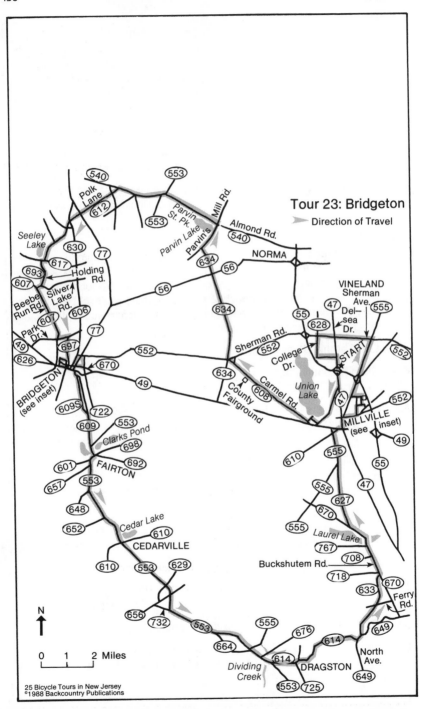

Tour 23: Bridgeton

Direction of Travel

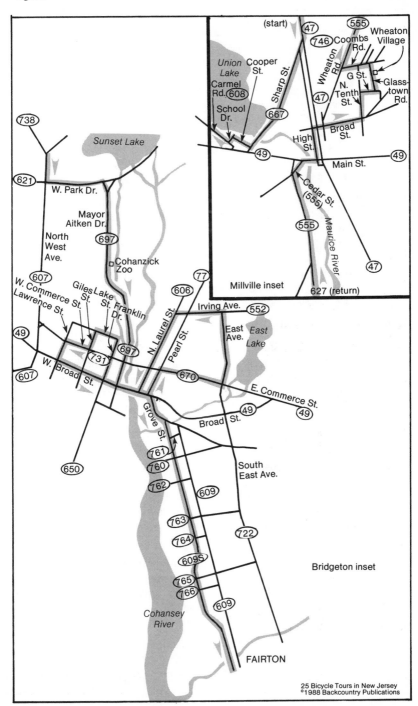

(start)

47
746 Coombs Rd.
555
Wheaton Village

Union Lake
Cooper St.
Carmel Rd. 608
School Dr.

Wheaton Rd.
G St.
N. Tenth St.
Glasstown Rd.

47

667

High St.

Broad St.

49
Main St.
49

Cedar St. (555)

555
Maurice River

Millville inset

47

627 (return)

738

Sunset Lake

621
W. Park Dr.

Mayor Aitken Dr.
697

North West Ave.
Cohanzick Zoo

607
W. Commerce St.
Lawrence St.
Giles St.
Lake St.
Franklin Dr.

77
606
Irving Ave.
552

East Ave.
East Lake

49
731
697
N. Laurel St.
Pearl St.

607
W. Broad St.
670
E. Commerce St.

650
Grove St.
Broad St.
49
49

761
760
South East Ave.

762
609

763
722

764

609S
Bridgeton inset

765
766
609

Cohansey River

FAIRTON

25 Bicycle Tours in New Jersey
©1988 Backcountry Publications

an unusual "lion" water fountain, if you have to refill your canteen. The zoo has a small, but interesting collection of animals grouped together according to their geographic ranges.

The Nail Museum, former office of the Cumberland Nail and Iron Works, is about a mile down the road. In its heyday around 1815, the company employed several hundred people for the production of wrought iron nails until these were displaced in the 1890s by the less expensive wire nail.

Glance left as you approach West Commerce Street; this complex of buildings, known locally as the Seven Sisters, contains some of the oldest commercial structures in New Jersey.

25.9   RIGHT on West Commerce Street.

Bridgeton, reputed to be New Jersey's largest historic district, has more than 2,000 houses and buildings on the National Register of Historic Places. Many of the Colonial, Federalist, and Victorian houses, built in the 1700s, are still in use today.

As you turn into Commerce Street, note the bright yellow Federal building at 31 West Commerce; built by David Sheppard in 1791 as his private residence, it is the oldest mansion in town.

26.0   RIGHT on Franklin Drive.

26.1   LEFT on Lake Street.

Rather than chop down a giant oak, it was left standing in the street. Pedal around it and stop at 25 Lake Street. Built in Gothic Revival style in 1872, this house, known as The House of Seven Gables, served in the past as a private school and maternity hospital; it is now an apartment residence.

26.2   LEFT on Giles Street.

26.3   RIGHT at the stop sign on West Commerce Street.

The eclectic Victorian house on the right at 137 West Commerce Street, now a funeral home, was built in the 1870s. Its roof is Second Empire, the windows Italianate, the doorway is Colonial Revival, and the porch is Greek Revival.

26.5   LEFT on Lawrence Street.

Lock your bike onto the iron gate in front of the First Presbyterian Church on the right just beyond the intersection with Broad Street, and take a few minutes to wander among the interesting ancient tombstones in its adjacent cemetery.

26.6   LEFT on West Broad Street.

At the courthouse, on the right, you'll find the bell that rang out to summon people for a formal reading of the Declaration of Independence on July 7, 1776, and to witness the burning of the emblem of

British rule. Across the street stands Potter's Tavern, built in 1767, with architecture typical of frame houses built in New Jersey during the seventeenth and eighteenth centuries. The tavern served as a meeting place where people talked of liberty and separation from British rule and where the first issue of the *Plain Dealer* was posted. This paper, New Jersey's first, ran for several issues.

27.2 **LEFT on Pearl Street.**

27.3 **RIGHT on East Commerce Street.**
More than 20,000 arrow points, spears, pots, and shards from the Lenni-Lenape Indians who once lived in the area can be examined at the Woodruff Museum, housed in the basement of the library on the right in 0.1 mile. (Open 1 to 4 p.m. weekdays, but sometimes the librarian will open it upon request; there is no admission fee.)

27.7 **LEFT on (unmarked) East Avenue.**
If you see East Lake on your left, you've gone too far. There are several historic houses here, including the one at 69 East Avenue, built in 1833 by the mayor of Bridgeton.

28.1 **LEFT on Irving Avenue.**

28.4 **LEFT on (unmarked) North Laurel Street.**
There is a lot more to see in Bridgeton. We suggest that you find a place to stay and explore more of the historic district by foot. Have dinner, get a good night's sleep, and start out early the next morning. We recommend the Cohansey Hotel, a Victorian inn in the center of town. It offers comfortable rooms, stores bicycles inside a locked storeroom, serves a free continental breakfast, and allows up to five people to share a room. The management promises a discount if you mention this book. It is located at Broad and Laurel Streets; telephone (609) 455-8600.

28.8 **LEFT on East Broad Street.**

28.9 **RIGHT on Grove Street at sign for Fairton, just past the sheriff's office.**

30.6 **Bear RIGHT on Route 609.**
The Cohanzick Country Club's golf course is on the right in about a half mile; it's open to the public.

31.8 **Bear RIGHT on Route 553.**
You'll cross Clarks Pond, a scenic spot.

32.2 **RIGHT at the "T" on Route 692, then LEFT on Route 553 south.**
This rough road has light traffic and passes farms and produce stands. Cedar Lake (in the town of Cedarville) appears at 35.9 miles on the left and has an inviting swimming beach. Food and drinks are available in town; there's an ice-cream stand at 38.9 miles.

At 39.6 miles, follow the main road to the left as Route 732 veers to the right. A swampy pond becomes visible on the right in a couple of miles, and you'll cross a bridge over Dividing Creek at 43.7 miles.

43.9   **LEFT after the bridge on Route 614 to Dragston.**
In 1.1 miles, follow the road by turning left and then right immediately after.

47.8   **LEFT at the "T" on North Avenue (Route 649).**

48.0   **STRAIGHT ahead as Route 649 veers off to the right.**
Continue straight at 49.4 miles as Ferry Road leads to the right. You'll be entering a forested area.

50.8   **LEFT at the "T" on (unmarked) Buckshutem Road (Route 670).**
The headquarters for the Edward G. Bevan Fish and Wildlife Management Area is to your right as you turn. Opportunities for purchasing food or drink are just ahead. At 52.2 miles cross Laurel Lake, a peaceful spot for a break.

52.9   **RIGHT on (unmarked) Route 627 at the sign for Millville.**

55.5   **STRAIGHT ahead on Route 555 north.**
This road takes you into Millville.

56.6   **RIGHT on Cedar Street (Route 555).**

56.8   **RIGHT at the "T" on Main Street.**
Before crossing the Maurice River, you'll come to a convenience store. Riverfront Park is another pleasant place to relax.

57.1   **LEFT on High Street.**
Shops of all kinds line Millville's main street.

57.5   **RIGHT on Broad Street.**

58.2   **LEFT on North 10th Street.**
A small store here has snacks and ice cream.

58.5   **RIGHT on G Street.**

58.7   **LEFT on Glasstown Road.**
Turn right into the circular driveway in front of the entrance to Wheaton Village at 59.0 miles and chain your bike to the fence.

The minute you enter Wheaton Village, you'll leave the twentieth century behind, for the buildings, streets, and shops within are a recreation of the styles prevalent in the late 1800s. Inside the impressive Museum of American Glass is a collection of more than 7,000 objects ranging from paperweights to fiber optics, Mason jars, and Tiffany masterpieces. Here you'll learn how glass is made and the history of Wheaton Village, which dates back to 1888.

In the Glass Factory, you'll feel the heat from the 2,100 degree Fahrenheit furnace as you watch artisans scoop up blobs of molten glass on long rods and shape the oozing fiery balls into magnificent colored shapes. As you watch this fascinating process, you'll hear how it's done as well. For a fee of $35, you can arrange to make your own colored flower paperweight under the supervision of a glassmaker.

Train buffs can take a short ride aboard the half-scale replica of an 1863 C. P. Huntington train. Or, if you're into crafts, you can watch tinsmith demonstrations, a potter making traditional hand thrown and decorated saltglazed wares, and woodmaking and lampmaking projects.

Before leaving, visit the print shop, have an ice cream at the Victorian-era pharmacy counter, and see the collection of nostalgic items at the General Store. On the way out you'll probably see Professor Elias B. Fester holding his medicine show or riding his Boneshaker highwheeler. He usually welcomes questions from fellow cyclists. (Open daily April through December from 10 a.m. to 5 p.m., January through March closed Monday and Tuesday, and closed New Year's, Easter, Thanksgiving, and Christmas; there is an admission fee. Call (609) 825-6800 for information on special events.)

When you're finished, continue around the driveway to the right.

59.2   RIGHT on Glasstown Road.

59.3   LEFT at the "T" on Coombs Road.

59.7   RIGHT at the "T" on Route 555, Wheaton Road.
Be careful on this wide street as you cross the ramps leading to and from Route 55.

62.1   LEFT on Sherman Avenue (Route 552).
Cycling is easy along this wide road.

64.5   LEFT on Route 628.
Cumberland County College, on the right at about 64.8 miles, is in a lovely setting surrounded by pine trees.

65.6   RIGHT on Route 47.
There are lots of stores along this stretch.

66.0   RIGHT into the K-Mart Shopping Center.

Bicycle shops:
Green Acres Bike Shop, Route 49, Millville, (609) 455-7531.
Millville Tire Service, 225 North High Street, Millville, (609) 825-5555.
Ruberti's Bicycles, 603 Chestnut Avenue, Vineland, (609) 691-5853.
S & R Schwinn Sales, 3419 South Delsea Drive, Vineland, (609) 327-1311.
Tommy's Bicycles, Almond Road, Norma, (609) 692-9146.

24

Belleplain

Location: Cape May County
Starting point: Cedar Square Center, Route 9, Seaville
Terrain: Flat
Traffic: Light
Round-trip distance pedaled: 30.0 miles
Highlights: Belleplain State Forest, swimming, fishing.

Northern Cape May County is a rural area well endowed with fragrant pine forests and charming byways. Along most of this trip you'll experience complete solitude, especially in the pristine woods found in Belleplain State Forest. Here you can relax and swim in Lake Nummy's cool, clean water or picnic under the shade of fragrant pines.

There is very little traffic on this trip, and because most of the roads have a shoulder, you'll be able to spend more time concentrating on the scenery.

Leave your car at the parking lot of the Jamesway Department Store at Cedar Square Center on Route 9 in Seaville, just north of the intersection with State Route 50. Reset your odometer at the exit from the shopping center where it meets Route 9.

0.0   **LEFT (south) on Route 9.**
      Traffic can be somewhat heavy here at times, but the road and shoulder are wide. Ice cream, drinks, and groceries are available at 2.7 miles. Magnolia Lake, on the right at 3.0 miles, is a beautiful spot to stop for a moment or two.

3.3   **RIGHT on Main Street (Route 628).**

4.6   **LEFT at the sign for South Dennis, continuing on Route 628.**

7.4   **RIGHT on Route 83.**
      There is a custard stand just after this turn.

8.1   **RIGHT on Route 47.**
      Route 47 is a main highway, but it has a wide shoulder most of the way. There is a food market at 8.8 miles, just before two jewel-like ponds come into view on the right.

10.8   **RIGHT on Route 557 (Washington Avenue).**

11.3   **LEFT on Pine Swamp Road.**

In spite of ruts and potholes, this road is easy to negotiate. You may see an occasional bicyclist in this section thickly wooded with oak and pine. Go slowly; deer, fox, cottontail, opossum, squirrels, muskrats, and beavers frequently dart out of the woods onto the roadway.

14.6   LEFT into Belleplain State Forest Recreation Area.
Established in 1928 for public recreation, timber production, wildlife management, and conservation of water, Belleplain State Forest was named in honor of the last Lenni-Lenape chief to rule in Cape May County. Its stands of pine, oak, and southern white cedar are a feast for the eyes.

Lake Nummy is on the right at 14.9 miles. The park office can supply a map of the park and has rest rooms.

15.1   RIGHT on the park road just past the lake.
You'll arrive at the lakefront beach area in about 0.1 mile. This is a great place for picnicking, swimming, or just taking a nice break amid the trees. When you're ready, follow the park road and go around the barricade that is at 15.5 miles. Many branches are strewn along this path. In about one-half mile you'll reach a second barricade; go around this one, too.

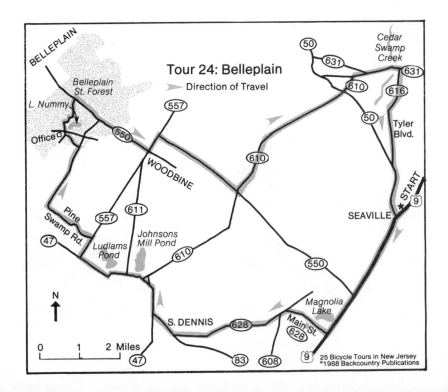

Tour 24: Belleplain
Direction of Travel

25 Bicycle Tours in New Jersey
©1988 Backcountry Publications

16.0   RIGHT at the "T" on Route 550.

A seven-mile road marker is visible just after you turn. This excellent road skirts along Belleplain State Forest for about 1.5 miles. Route 550 turns LEFT at 18.1 miles as it is joined by Route 557 and then continues RIGHT at 18.5 miles. Soon after, you'll come to Lincoln Park, a local recreation area, and a market.

Fishing is one way to relax at Belleplain State Forest.

20.9   LEFT at the stoplight on Route 610.

Oaks and pines line this wide road. At 24.4 miles, you'll pass a church
built in 1853 and a large cemetery.

24.4   Bear RIGHT on Route 631.

This smooth road passes through a swampy area with high grasses
and dozens of red-winged blackbirds. Cedar Swamp Creek, formed
when underground springs of fresh water broke through the soil in
what was previously an ocean floor, is at 26.1 miles. Masses of white
cedar eventually took over the rich, moist soil, providing a perfect
habitat for wildlife.

26.2   RIGHT on Route 616 (Tyler Boulevard).

Fortunately this rough, shoulderless road has little traffic.

28.5   LEFT at the "T" on Route 50.

An ice-cream shop, food market, and several restaurants can be
found in this area.

29.9   LEFT on Route 9.

Arrive at the entrance to Cedar Square Center at 30.0 miles.

Bicycle shops:
There are none along this route.

25

Cape May

Location: Cape May County
Starting point: Cape May County Park
Terrain: Flat
Traffic: Moderate
Round-trip distance pedaled: 40.3 miles
Highlights: Victorian houses, beaches, swimming, lighthouse, Cold Spring Village, Wetlands Institute, Cape May "diamonds."

Cape May, one of the oldest seaside resorts on the Atlantic Coast, once attracted such notables as Abraham Lincoln, Franklin Pierce, James Buchanan, and Ulysses S. Grant. In 1903, Henry Ford entered his car in beach races here, trying (unsuccessfully) to lure people into buying stock in his new company. The area is also recognized as an outstanding bird-watching spot, where more than 400 species of birds, including peregrine falcons, bald eagles, and osprey, can be seen during their spring and fall migrations.

Although this trip is only 40.3 miles long, it includes quite a few places of interest. If you want to linger at some, spend time swimming, or hunt for Cape May "diamonds," consider taking two days. (Write to the Cape May Chamber of Commerce, Box 74, Cape May Court House, N.J. 08210 for a list of hotels and bed-and-breakfast inns.)

Begin at Cape May County Park, located on Route 9 about a mile north of Cape May Court House. The park offers picnicking facilities and a small zoo with 100 animals. Special events and concerts are sponsored here during the summer.

Park your car, pedal to the park entrance on Route 9 and reset your odometer.

0.0   RIGHT (south) on Route 9.

The Cape May County Museum, located 0.2 mile on the left, contains Indian relics, old tools, household utensils, and artifacts relating to Cape May's early history. (Open September through December and March through June; there is an admission fee.)

1.1   LEFT on Route 657.

After crossing the Garden State Parkway, you'll be riding on a wide shoulder next to heavy traffic, especially during the summer tourist season. The road is lined with tall grasses and marshland. After crossing the wooden bridge at 2.3 miles, look for the Wetlands Institute, which is housed in a lighthouse-shaped building on the right.

3.0   RIGHT into the Institute's parking lot.

A film about the surrounding salt marshes and an explanation on their ecological importance is presented at regular intervals. There is also a self-guiding Salt Marsh Trail showing the effects the harsh marsh environment has on plants and animals. Climb the spiral stairs to the observation tower for a bird's-eye view of the 6,000-acre marshland and surrounding communities. A rest room and water fountain are in the building. (Open May 15 to October 15 daily, and Tuesday, Thursday, and Saturday from October 15 to May 15. There is an admission fee.)

When finished, continue east on Route 657, crossing the bridge into Stone Harbor. Food is available here.

3.8   RIGHT on Route 619 (Third Avenue) at the sign for Wildwood and Cape May.

Great Channel, part of the Inland Waterway, is to the right; the 21-acre Stone Harbor Bird Sanctuary is on the left at 4.6 miles. Visitors are not admitted, but you can spot birds with binoculars as they fly overhead.

Continuing straight ahead, you'll cross a bridge at 5.2 miles; it affords excellent views of marshland, water, and fishing boats. There's room at the end of the bridge if you want to pull over to the side of the road to watch shorebirds and herons feed in the salt marshes to the right. At 6.8 miles, you'll cross another bridge; even cyclists must pay the toll.

7.2   LEFT at the "T" on Route 147 toward Wildwood.

You'll find lots of restaurants here. In a short distance, you'll cross a rickety wooden bridge and encounter a good deal of traffic, but thankfully there's a wide shoulder. Route 147 zigzags as you approach Wildwood. Follow signs for Cape May.

8.7   RIGHT on First Avenue.

8.8   LEFT on New York Avenue.

Marinas are on the right.

9.4   RIGHT on 13th Avenue.

9.5   LEFT on Delaware Avenue.

Water and rest rooms are available at 9.9 miles within the park.

10.1   LEFT on 26th Street.

10.6   RIGHT on Atlantic Avenue.

This main drag has many motels and restaurants. The beach and boardwalk are to the left. (A beach use fee is charged.)

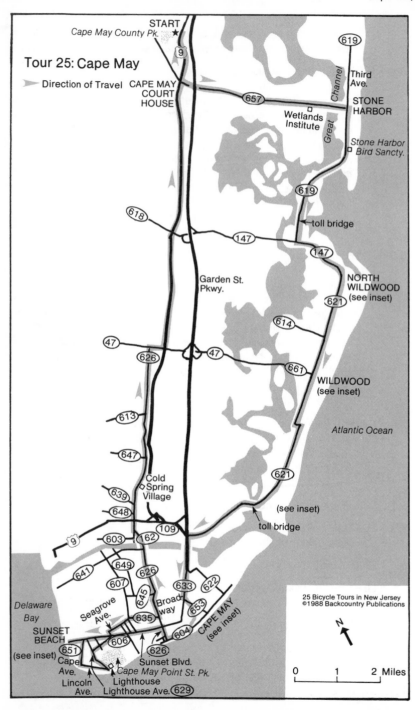

Tour 25: Cape May

Direction of Travel

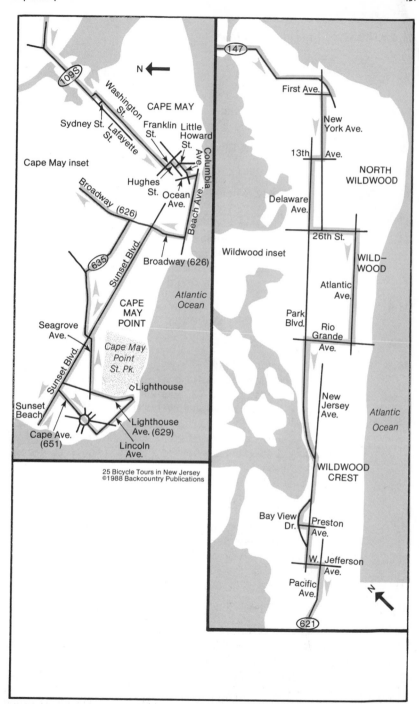

CAPE MAY

109S

Washington St.

Sydney St. Lafayette St.

Cape May inset

Franklin St. Little Howard St.

Columbia Ave.

Hughes St. Ocean Ave.

Broadway (626)

Beach Ave.

635

Sunset Blvd.

Broadway (626)

CAPE MAY POINT

Atlantic Ocean

Seagrove Ave.

Cape May Point St. Pk.

Lighthouse

Sunset Blvd.

Sunset Beach

Cape Ave. (651)

Lighthouse Ave. (629)

Lincoln Ave.

25 Bicycle Tours in New Jersey
©1988 Backcountry Publications

147

First Ave.

New York Ave.

13th Ave.

NORTH WILDWOOD

Delaware Ave.

26th St.

Wildwood inset

WILD–WOOD

Atlantic Ave.

Park Blvd.

Rio Grande Ave.

New Jersey Ave.

Atlantic Ocean

WILDWOOD CREST

Bay View Dr. Preston Ave.

W. Jefferson Ave.

Pacific Ave.

621

11.6   RIGHT on Rio Grande Avenue.

12.0   LEFT on Park Boulevard.
> A selection of fast food places is at the intersection. Excursion and fishing boats are on the right at 12.7 miles.

13.2   RIGHT on New Jersey Avenue.
> Sailboat rentals are available by the hour here.

13.4   Bear RIGHT on Bay View Drive.

13.8   LEFT on Preston Avenue.

13.9   RIGHT on New Jersey Avenue.

14.3   LEFT on West Jefferson Avenue.

14.4   RIGHT on Pacific Avenue (Route 621).
> If you need supplies, try the grocery in 0.2 mile. Have change ready for another toll bridge at 15.7 miles. This nautical stretch passes by seafood markets, restaurants, and a yacht basin.

17.4   LEFT at the "T" at the sign for Cape May onto Route 109 South.
> Use caution at this busy intersection.

18.2   LEFT on Sidney Street.

18.3   RIGHT on Washington Street.
> Cape May, designated as a National Historic Landmark, has more than 600 buildings dating from more than one hundred years ago. Architectural buffs will appreciate the variety of cupolas. Supposedly the "captain's walk" cupola facing the sea was used by wives who watched for their husband's returning ship, and the "widow's walk" was an open area on the roof used as a retreat for the wives who had watched in vain.
>
> Stop at the Emlen Physick House at 1050 Washington Street for a tour of this 16-room mansion, designed in the Stick style in 1878. Inside is a collection of Victorian furniture, toys, tools, and costumes. Next door, in the former carriage house, you can examine the latest exhibit on display by the Cape May County Art League, fill your canteen, or use the restroom. (Open daily except Friday; there is an admission fee to the Physick House only.) You'll pass another ornate Victorian house at 720 Washington Street.

19.1   LEFT on Franklin Street.

19.2   RIGHT on Hughes Street.
> The houses on this street have many interesting features; look for the dormer windows at 655 Hughes Street and the brightly painted gingerbread at 654 Hughes.

19.3 **LEFT on Little Howard Street, then RIGHT on Columbia Avenue.**
Numerous bed-and-breakfast inns line Columbia Avenue. The impressive house at 635 Columbia Avenue was built in 1856 as a club for southern gentlemen. If you're interested in seeing more of these charming houses, cycle up and down the local streets because the route will now follow the ocean.

19.4 **LEFT on (unmarked) Ocean Avenue.**

19.5 **RIGHT on Beach Avenue.**
Hotels and restaurants are jammed during summer months. If you want to take a dip, bike racks are available at each beach entry. (There is a fee for using the beach.)

20.2 **RIGHT on Broadway (Route 626).**

20.5 **LEFT on Sunset Boulevard (Route 606).**

22.7 **STOP at the dead end.**
You've reached Sunset Beach, the favorite hunting grounds for those who search the sands for quartz pebbles known as Cape May diamonds. That weird, partially submerged hulk in front of you is the Atlantus, an experimental concrete ship that was towed here after it partially sank in a storm in 1926. It was one of 14 built during World War I.
After filling your bags with diamonds, turn back on Route 606.

23.1 **RIGHT on Cape Avenue, Route 651.**
Stay on Cape Avenue around the traffic circle.

23.7 **LEFT at the end of the street on Lincoln Avenue.**
You'll be riding along the edge of large sand dunes.

24.2 **LEFT at the end of the street on Lighthouse Avenue, Route 629.**
Cape May Point Lighthouse, one of the oldest lighthouses still actively commissioned by the Coast Guard as a navigational aide, dates to 1859 and stands 165 feet above ground level. Its light, visible for 19 miles, goes on automatically at 4:30 p.m. daily.

24.3 **RIGHT into Cape May Point State Park.**
This is a great place to sit and listen to the pounding surf. The park offers picnicking, rest rooms, and a three-mile walking trail through a natural area.
When you're ready, follow the one-way signs out of the park.

24.6 **RIGHT on Lighthouse Avenue.**

25.0 **RIGHT on Seagrove Avenue.**
Cross Sunset Boulevard at 25.5 miles.

26.1   STRAIGHT ahead on Route 635.

26.8   LEFT on Route 626 (Broadway).
Drinks are available along this road. You'll cross Route 9 at 29.0 miles before coming to the Cold Spring Presbyterian Church, built in 1823, and a huge cemetery.

29.7   RIGHT at the entrance to Historic Cold Spring Village.
Representing a typical nineteenth-century south Jersey farm village, all of these 15 structures were saved from destruction and brought here to create a live outdoor museum consisting of craft shops, a country store, and a restaurant. (Open daily from 10 a.m. to sunset, Memorial Day to the end of September; there is an admission fee.)

29.8   RIGHT (north) on Route 626.
A food market is at 31.8 miles.

33.0   RIGHT on Route 47.

33.3   LEFT (north) on Route 9.
Eating places abound at this intersection. Although Route 9 is a major artery further north, it is just a country road here. You'll pass the two-story wooden 1850 courthouse, for which the community of Cape May Court House is named, at 38.8 miles.
The entrance to Cape May County Park is at 40.3 miles.

Bicycle shops:

Hale Sports Cycling and Fitness, 5 Mechanic Street, Cape May Court House, (609) 465-3126.
Algie's Place, 114 East 17th Avenue, North Wildwood, (609) 729-5669.
Harbor Bike and Beach Shop, 9828 3rd Avenue, Stone Harbor, (609) 368-3691.

Appendix

National Organizations

Bicycle USA/League of American Wheelmen, 6707 Whitestone Road, Suite 209, Baltimore, MD 21207, (301) 944-3399.

A nationwide organization of bicyclists that promotes bicycling by sponsoring annual races and maintaining a directory of bicycle route maps. Annual membership fee $22; includes monthly publication "Bicycle USA."

American Youth Hostels, National Administrative Office, 1331 I Street, NW, Suite 800, Washington, DC 20005, (800) 424-9426.

A national organization that maintains a network of hostels and organizes bicycle trips. Annual membership $10 adults, youth, and senior citizens.

Bikecentennial, P.O. Box 8308, Missoula, MT 59807, (406) 721-1776.

A national bicycle touring and route information service. Annual membership $22; includes monthly publication.

Bicycling Books

The All New Complete Book of Bicycling, Sloane, (Simon & Schuster, New York, NY, 1981)

Everything you want to know about choosing, using, and maintaining a bicycle.

All-Terrain Bicycles, Sloane, (Fireside Press, Simon & Schuster, New York, NY, 1985)

Advice on choosing and using mountain bikes, including repair and riding techniques.

Anybody's Bike Book, Cuthbertson and Morall, (Ten Speed Press, Berkeley, CA, 1979)

An easy-to-read bicycle repair manual covering maintenance you can easily do by yourself.

Freewheeling, Bicycling the Open Road, Ferguson, (The Mountaineers, Seattle, WA, 1984)

Well-presented facts on choosing a bicycle, caring for it, food for the road, camping, and more.

John Marino's Bicycling Book, Marino, (Houghton Mifflin, New York, NY, 1981)

A basic guide to bicycling and physical fitness.

The Bike Bag Book, Cuthbertson, (Ten Speed Press, Berkeley, CA, 1986)
An amazingly tiny-sized book loaded with clear repair directions if you get stuck on the road.

Nature Books

A Field Guide to the Birds, Peterson, (Houghton Mifflin, Boston, MA, 1980)
For cyclists who want to identify the chirping overhead.

A Field Guide to Trees and Shrubs, Petrides, (Houghton Mifflin, Boston, MA, 1973)
Worth buying if you want to identify trees en route.

A Field Guide to Wildflowers of Northeastern North America, Peterson, (Houghton Mifflin, Boston, MA, 1974)
During spring months this book will be extremely helpful in identifying the bright carpet of wildflowers along your route.

A Practical Guide for the Amateur Naturalist, Durrell, (Knopf, New York, NY, 1982)
This beautifully written reference book will answer any questions you have about the birds, bees, flora, and fauna.

Birds of North America, Robbins, (Golden Press, New York, NY, 1983)
Learn how to identify the birds you encounter on these tours.

Complete Field Guide to North American Wildlife, (Eastern Edition, Harper & Row, New York, NY, 1981)
Very complete reference book with excellent illustrations.

Information on New Jersey

"New Jersey Bicycling Information," (c/o William Feldman, Bicycle Advocate, N.J. Department of Transportation, 1035 Parkway Avenue, Trenton, N.J. 08625.)
Information on bicycle clubs in New Jersey, addresses of county offices for maps, touring tips, and access restrictions.

The New Jersey House, Schwartz, (Rutgers University Press, New Brunswick, NJ, 1983)
Photographs and details on the architecturally interesting houses found in the state.

Passage Between Rivers, Menzies, (Rutgers University Press, New Brunswick, NJ, 1976)
Captioned photographs detailing the history of the Delaware and Raritan Canal.

The Pine Barrens, McPhee, (Ballantine Books, New York, NY, 1968)
A sentimental look at New Jersey's most mysterious region.

This is New Jersey, Cunningham, (Rutgers University Press, New Brunswick, NJ, 1978)

   All about the state's history, towns, historic sites, and counties.

Topographical Map of New Jersey, (Hubbard, 1946 Raymond Drive, Northbrook, Illinois 60062)

   A beautiful hard wall map available framed or unframed for reference.

New Jersey's Special Places, Zatz (The Countryman Press, Woodstock, Vermont, 1990).

   Fifty-two outings to New Jersey's most fascinating natural and historical attractions.

Index

Also from The Countryman Press and Backcountry Publications

The Countryman Press and Backcountry Publications, long known for fine books on travel and outdoor recreation, offer a range of practical and readable manuals.

Bicycling

Keep on Pedaling: The Complete Guide to Adult Bicycling, $12.95

Bicycle Touring Guides

25 Bicycle Tours on Delmarva, $9.95
25 Mountain Bike Tours in Massachusetts: From the Connecticut River to the Atlantic, $9.95
25 Bicycle Tours in Eastern Pennsylvania, $8.95
20 Bicycle Tours in the Finger Lakes, $8.95
20 Bicycle Tours in the Five Boroughs (NYC), $8.95
25 Bicycle Tours in the Hudson Valley, $9.95
25 Bicycle Tours in Maine, $9.95
25 Bicycle Tours in New Jersey, $9.95
20 Bicycle Tours in and around New York City, $7.95
25 Bicycle Tours in Ohio's Western Reserve, $11.95
25 Bicycle Tours in Vermont, $8.95
25 Mountain Bike Tours in Vermont, $9.95
25 Bicycle Tours in and around Washington, DC, $9.95

Other books of interest to New Jersey residents

New Jersey's Special Places, $12.95
Fifty Hikes in New Jersey, $11.95
Fifty Hikes in the Hudson Valley, $10.95
Fifty Hikes in Eastern Pennsylvania, $10.95

We offer many more books on hiking, walking, skiing, fishing and canoeing in New England, New York State, the Mid-Atlantic states, and the Midwest--plus books on travel, nature, and many other subjects.

Our titles are available in bookshops and in many sporting goods stores, or they may be ordered directly from the publisher. When ordering by mail, please add $2.50 per order for shipping and handling. To order or obtain a complete catalog, please write The Countryman Press, Inc., P.O. Box 175, Woodstock, Vermont 05091.